CONTACTS, OPPORTUNITIES, AND CRIMINAL ENTERPRISE

Success in criminal enterprise depends largely on the methods offenders employ in committing their crimes. An offender's pursuit of increasing financial returns and decreasing costs is mediated by the structure of his pool of useful and trustworthy connections. In *Contacts, Opportunities, and Criminal Enterprise*, Carlo Morselli examines how business-oriented criminals with extensive personal networks achieve and maintain competitive advantages in their financial activities and overall criminal careers.

Based on two case studies of criminal careers in international cannabis smuggling and Cosa Nosta racketeering, the book proposes a social network framework to study the underlying social relationships influencing achievement in crime. Morselli further utilizes this relational approach to illustrate how early success and long-term survival in criminal enterprise are achieved, and how criminals' networks of contacts and opportunities can insulate them from potentially career-damaging forces such as law enforcement and fellow criminals.

CARLO MORSELLI is a professor in the School of Criminology at l'Université de Montréal.

CARLO MORSELLI

Contacts, Opportunities, and Criminal Enterprise

UNIVERSITY OF TORONTO PRESS
Toronto Buffalo London

© University of Toronto Press Incorporated 2005
Toronto Buffalo London
Printed in Canada

ISBN 0-8020-3879-4 (cloth)
ISBN 0-8020-3811-5 (paper)

Printed on acid-free paper

Library and Archives Canada Cataloguing in Publication

Morselli, Carlo, 1969–
  Contacts, opportunities and criminal enterprise / Carlo Morselli.

  Includes bibliographical references and index.
  ISBN 0-8020-3879-4 (bound).   ISBN 0-8020-3811-5 (pbk.)

  1. Criminal behaviour.   2. Criminals – Social networks.   3. Criminal
  psychology.   4. Organized crime.   I. Title.

  HV6035.M67 2005   364.3   C2005-902067-9

This book has been published with the help of a grant from the Canadian
Federation for the Humanities and Social Sciences, through the Aid to
Scholarly Publications Programme, using funds provided by the Social
Sciences and Humanities Research Council of Canada.

University of Toronto Press acknowledges the financial assistance to its
publishing program of the Canada Council for the Arts and the Ontario
Arts Council.

University of Toronto Press acknowledges the financial support for its
publishing activities of the Government of Canada through the Book
Publishing Industry Development Program (BPIDP).

Contents

Acknowledgments

I have been guided by a host of friends, acquaintances, and respected others in developing various parts of this book. Most importantly, Pierre Tremblay was my alter ego throughout all phases of this study. His attentive listening, suggestive insights, and striving for creativity make this book as much Pierre's as it is mine. He is indeed a true mentor and friend.

Maurice Cusson also has a unique place in the present work, with his unrivalled passion for all that is crime and justice. His call for clarity and explicit reasoning in writing is heard (but not necessarily followed) by all who know him; his work ethic is unrelenting. Throughout the past years, I have been fortunate enough to witness this model of veracity on a daily basis.

I have read several works that are not incorporated extensively enough in this book – at least not in proportion to the impact they had on me. I never really learned how to credit various authors for their inspirational contribution. I feel their influence; I just do not know how to express it. The three most important misuses here are of Jack Katz's *Seductions of Crime*, Randall Collins' *The Sociology of Philosophies*, and John Padgett and Christopher Ansell's 'Robust Action and the Rise of the Medici, 1400–1434.' All three had an immense impact in showing me how far we could reach in our expressions and how broad-minded we may be in doing so. I cannot remember the number of times that I found myself thinking: 'We're allowed to *do that*?'

Many other people have left their marks to various extents. At a very early phase, Bonnie Erickson directed me towards Burt's *Structural Holes*. I have never since looked back to thank her. I also thank Amedeo Cottino, Tom Naylor, James Jacobs, Ron Burt, Mark Granovetter, Klaus von Lampe, Bill McCarthy, Frederick Desroches, and William Chambliss for their comments, criticisms, and encouragement as various segments of the book were in progress. I am also grateful to John Hagan, Jean-Paul Brodeur, Jean Trépanier, Edward Kleemans, Jeff Ferrell, Jeffrey McIllwain, and anonymous reviewers for their assessments of earlier versions of the complete manuscript in either its initial dissertation form or in the various renditions that followed.

Earlier versions of Chapters 4, 5, and 6 were published as articles in *Crime, Law, and Social Change* (35 [2001]: pp. 203–44; 39 [2003]: pp. 383–418). I am grateful to Kluwer Academic Publishers (now Springer), and in particular the journal's former editor Alan Block, for permission to use this material here. The Social Sciences and Humanities Research Council of Canada provided financial support with a doctoral scholarship during the late 1990s and a more recent grant from the Canadian Federation for the Humanities and Social Sciences in its Aid to Scholarly Publications Programme.

In pursuing the book's publication with the University of Toronto Press, I was fortunate enough to encounter Stephen Kotowych at the gate. His editorial support and guidance made this new venture very appreciable. I would also like to thank Terry Teskey, for her countless copy-editing suggestions, and managing editor Anne Laughlin, who helped guide me through the final phases of publication. I thank Benoit Dupont for key time-saving advice during these last moments.

Finally, this book is dedicated to Fabienne, Béatrice, and Luca, who gave me a wonderful home to run back to.

CONTACTS, OPPORTUNITIES, AND
CRIMINAL ENTERPRISE

Introduction

I began this study during the mid-1990s with the intention to develop an understanding of social networks within the area of organized crime. At that early point, I mistakenly assumed that studying organized crime would lead me to criminal structures that were formally organized, that provided immensely prosperous opportunities for members, and that employed violent and forceful methods of control. My review of the research within this area and a variety of case analyses have taught me otherwise. One of the first things that you learn when you approach the growing research surrounding organized crime and analogous areas is that things are not as formally organized or elaborate as they seem to be. Indeed, since the early 1970s the main thread that has linked most of these studies is the questioning and critique of the standard stereotypes surrounding organized crime.

What has emerged from these past studies, however, is not neatly sorted into a common analytical line of inquiry. Competing concepts have emerged to denote particular systems or processes of criminal co-participation. Hence, some continue to discuss the issue in terms of 'organized crime,' while others have avoided this more popular term, perceiving it as too closely aligned with earlier images of criminal syndicates. New notions, such as 'illegal enterprise,' 'organizing crime,' and 'criminal enterprise', have been introduced as alternatives. Competing perspectives ranging from the traditional bureaucratic approach to the classical economic approach also developed around specific terms. This study proposes to merge these seemingly different perspectives within a more general rubric employing three basic concepts that, together, yield an analytical framework that enables us to cut across diverging outlooks. The framework is also applicable to the wider array of offenders that have been the subject of more extensive research in criminology (beyond the organized crime label).

Contacts

How others influence and shape an individual's criminal livelihood is the principal concern of this study. From the start, my aim was quite straightforward: to find a way to converge on a set of contacts surrounding a given individual and extract the various network designs and properties that sustain participation in crime. I am interested in networks that are built for crime not only because understanding such social forms in greater detail and from new angles will reveal a key foundation for the onset of a criminal career, but also for the direction and achievement level of the trajectory that follows. The incentive to focus on others is firmly entrenched within a sociology-of-crime tradition that has confronted its share of criticism since Sutherland's early formulations, but that has also experienced a revival throughout the past decade, particularly in reaction to the explicit rejection of the idea of organization and crime by some key criminologists.

This line of inquiry is facilitated by the social network or relational perspective that has been devoted to studying the place and influence of others in various facets of life. Studying how people collaborate in competitive environments and how networks form around a certain activity or throughout a person's career allows the researcher to uncover some of the basic assets of any individual's life. The approach does not, however, suggest that contacts, networks, or social capital 'count' in any hard, deterministic way. Instead, and in the spirit of Cullen's (1983) structuring approach to crime, such surrogates of the relational foundations of life are perceived as contingencies that 'shape' outcomes and transitions. Contacts are, in brief, pivotal to an individual's criminal experience.

Opportunities

One of the key contributions that contacts provide to any given offender is access to a set of opportunities for crime. While the basic criminological approach to criminal opportunities has highlighted the more spontaneous and largely unplanned opportunities, the purposive action framework that is used throughout this study to sketch the criminal experience as a goal-oriented pursuit is derived from both rational choice approaches to crime and a series of network studies on conventional social mobility and competition. Social network research allows us to expand on the more prosperous uses of available criminal opportunities. This focus is indeed intentional on my part, and is set within a wider research program on criminal achievement. Following Sutherland (1937) and with additional inspiration from Katz (1988), this larger program is designed to highlight the favourable foreground of criminal experiences.

In the present book, I offer a case study approach in advancing the network segment of this criminal achievement program. By relying on the personal accounts of two men who, over twenty-five years, endured and progressed in their respective criminal careers, I seek to understand how one endures and prospers – gets ahead, so to speak – through crime. These cases are adequate counterparts to Shover's (1996) persistent thieves, who seemingly gained very little during their long-term experiences in crime. The selection of cases is strategic and intended to shed light on structured opportunists in crime. After all, what better way do we have to understand crime than to study those who made a life out of it? This inquiry leads to a series of propositions built around the ideas of entrepreneurial networks and privileged positioning. I suggest that the relational strengths emerging from this study's cases are lacking within the scope of Shover's career criminals and the considerable majority of crime participants that have been the predominant concern of criminologists working within a control framework.

Criminal Enterprise

The two criminal career cases I consider are entrenched within illegal markets or elaborate co-offending settings. This restriction is not meant to discount the framework's pertinence for less sophisticated and non-mercantile crime contexts. As mentioned earlier, the rationale for selecting such cases was largely the length of the careers and the achievement levels they attained.

Studying the twists and turns of long-term experiences in crime offers a better chance of identifying those network patterns that are useful for crime. Typical short-term or sporadic experiences in crime, although representative of many offenders, are not as likely to be advanced in relational terms. The typical criminal career is therefore not a useful starting point for someone looking to identify the relational foundations of sustained and relatively successful criminal careers. On the other hand, the organized crime or criminal enterprise field of research is quite conducive to the more common forms of money-oriented crime, in that there is a clear continuum between criminal market participants who act as individual entrepreneurs without any exclusive adhesion to a particular criminal group and those entrepreneurs who are members of an established criminal organization. Hence, the inclusion of both independent criminal entrepreneurs and members of criminal organizations renders social organization a variable in such settings. The principle assets that are established across such a continuum could subsequently be applied and tested across a wider set of money-oriented offenders who display various levels of organization and criminal achievement. Criminal entrepreneurs, whether within criminal markets, organized crime settings, or a variety of less consensual crime venues, seek to expand their networks by connecting with others in one or more business settings. Connecting with others expands their own pool of potential opportunities. How one connects with others influences the scope and form of the criminal experience.

In short, this study establishes how participation, advancement, and endurance in both independent and organized contexts of criminal enterprise may be firmly observed and subsequently understood by converging on the influence of key contacts throughout such experiences. Subcultural theories of crime may grasp the normative worlds that allow common-minded members of society to gather within a fixed social setting. Classical economic theories of crime may reveal the goal-oriented motivations and market-based actions driving atomistic players within specific arenas of competition. Traditional organizational theories of organized crime are effective in illustrating how some offenders unite in formal and hierarchical groupings in order to increase their efficiency and security. The strength of a network framework for criminal enterprise is that it converges on the process that allows one to become a criminal entrepreneur as well as maintaining and improving on that status. This process guides the entrepreneur in learning and complying with the normative aspects of a particular business world. This process also allows us to see how and why an entrepreneur's business activities or crimes are structured the way they are.

The analysis throughout the greater part of the study focuses on where past criminal entrepreneurs went with their careers and how the structure of their personal networks surrounding various outcomes and transitions figured throughout their personal trajectories. Without the network, both independent and organizationally entrenched criminal entrepreneurs lose the necessary vehicle that accompanies their drift away from conventional activities and guides them towards earning activities that are necessarily lodged within clandestine and often criminal working settings. These working settings are overlapping personal networks. Connecting with another's network offers potential access to that person's direct and indirect resources, as well as providing that person with access to one's own personal resources. Positioning within this relational world and its inherent asymmetries is what criminal stratification is built on.

Thriving criminal entrepreneurs may be few in number, but their rarity does not detract from their importance amongst a more general set of participants in crime. Stratification is common in most career areas. Collins (1998), for example, illustrates this within the scientific community, which has its own share of variation in personal creativity, emotional energy, advantageous mentoring, and networking strategies. The floating population that embraces intellectual circles consists primarily of 'transients' (the 75–80 per cent who contribute one or a few publications), followed by slightly more successful 'outer core' participants (20 per cent). The 'inner core' or 'top producers' (the 'crème') represent only 1–2 per cent of the floating population of active scholars, while the 'scientific stars' (the 'crème de la crème'), reports Collins, appear in only 'small absolute numbers' (see pp. 42–46). Transposing a similar stratification classification to the criminal population is not yet feasible in terms of identifying clear proportions, but it is quite clear that criminological research has been more concerned with the transient segment of juvenile or more sporadic offenders that have been the principal focus in the more general theories of crime. While the long-term aim of a criminal achievement theory of crime is to work towards a more general understanding of crime, its starting point is from the top and not the bottom.

The experiences of the individuals studied here may not be at all representative of the average career in crime and even less representative of the typical criminal experience. Successful offenders, however, do function as a model category for the aspirations of others who see crime as a plausible alternative for making a living. Whether others act on these aspirations is, once again, partly a matter of relationally oriented capacity. This relational capacity can no longer be overlooked by criminologists.

The Book's Structure

I have tried, as much as possible, to keep the book's format consistent with the manner in which the research developed. Chapter 1 is meant to situate the reader within the conceptual discrepancies that emerge from past research on organized crime and criminal enterprise. My position within this discussion is revealed, as are the various assumptions that guide the remainder of this study.

Chapter 2 presents the network framework that is at the centre of this book. It is developed along insights emerging from both purposive action frameworks for network analyses and organized crime research on Mafia and other groups. Burt's (1992) structural hole theory serves as the transit between these two fields. His theory was essential in developing this study because of its accent on both networks and achievement.

Chapter 3 provides the data sources and methodology used for the analytical portions of the book. I have come to realize that not all readers are interested in such chapters. Those who are not interested in possible replications of the developed method or in scrutinizing the chapters that follow are advised to pass over Chapter 3.

Chapters 4 and 5 apply the developed framework in quite different criminal career settings. Two case studies are presented. The first (in Chapter 4) centres on the career of Howard 'Mr. Nice' Marks, who was an active participant in the international cannabis trade from the late 1960s to his arrest in Spain in 1988. Although Marks often worked with the same co-participants, the structuring of his activities typified the short-term, opportunistic action groups that consistently emerge from studies on the distribution of illegal goods and services. He is our *independent criminal entrepreneur*.

A second case study (Chapter 5) focuses on the career of Sammy 'the Bull' Gravano, who, in contrast to the independent Marks, practiced his trade within the organizational confines of the Gambino family, one of New York City's five reputed Cosa Nostra families. Gravano, whose career spanned approximately the same time period as Marks' and ended with his arrest in 1990, ascended to the second-highest rank in the Gambino family (as underboss) while, at the same time, expanding his business activities as a racketeer in New York City's construction industry. He is our *organizationally bounded criminal entrepreneur*.

Although Marks' and Gravano's criminal experiences were distinct, both were relationally oriented. The bridge between the independent and organizational criminal entrepreneur becomes possible when we focus on the fact that these participants were, above all, network players par excellence. Understanding such relational dynamics also allows us to situate the place of prestige, power, and violence across criminal careers (see Chapter 6).

The final chapter provides a general wrap-up, as well as presenting a series of statements and extensions that emerge from the overall inquiry and proposing a research agenda.

1 Conceptual Discrepancies

Much work has been devoted to distinguishing between criminal (or illegal) enterprise and organized crime. Rather than pursue this debate, I have chosen to fuse the two and use them interchangeably. The studies advancing this debate have not convinced me that such distinctions warrant the creation of alternative concepts. Aside from apparent discrepancies between the organizational levels of working groups, their geographic and market scope, and the popularized threat that they are alleged to present, the idea of criminal enterprise is very much akin to that of organized crime.

For comparative purposes, take the distinction that Naylor (1997) makes between predatory crime and enterprise crime. In this case, the creation of a conceptual divide is indeed warranted. While the set of activities falling within the scope of predatory crime involves the redistribution of existing wealth that is generally bilaterally extracted from unwilling and clearly identifiable victims, activities falling under the enterprise crime heading imply the supply of new goods and services that takes place within a system of multilateral exchanges with consenting members of society. Yet if we attempt to create a similar divide between enterprise crime and organized crime, the search for exclusive referents brings us into the criminal marketplace with variations in the extent of criminal conspiracy and market domination, both of which have yet to be established on a consistent basis by any research. Naylor is right in maintaining that any similarity between criminal businesses and criminal organizations (of the Mafia type) is indeed 'fuzzy' (p. 15); however, such ambiguity does not merit the creation of a conceptual distinction. Quite differently, what we have is a continuum within the scope of criminal enterprise settings.

Naylor's work offers a useful guideline in that this variation could be worked out within the scope of an inclusive concept. As he also maintains, if a problem exists anywhere in terms of conceptual clarification, it is in regard to the conventional view of organized crime and the hasty policies or collateral damages that extend from them. The problem with the conventional view of organized crime is that the stereotypes emerging from it are too often superimposed on a wide array of criminal activities on the basis of a mere assumption. This is most obvious in the overt reference to such stereotypes in law enforcement settings, media outlets, and public circles.

If the notion of organized crime is inflated in popular and official settings, its use in scholarly research in this area is perhaps too restrictive. 'Organized crime' is primarily used when bureaucratic-like and more elaborate organizations are identified. This appears to be rarely the case. 'Criminal enterprise' or 'illegal enterprise' is generally used to denote those activities, processes, or organizational forms that are more informal and flexible. Hence, while the official and popular view of organized crime systematically assumes formal sophistication and criminal marketplace domination across too many criminal settings, much scholarly research, driven by the attempt to correct such misperceptions, has erred in the inverse direction. The result is that research on organized crime, illegal enterprise, organizing crime, syndicate crime, and a multitude of other notions offered to denote what falls within the scope of criminal enterprise is tainted by collective ambiguity[1] (Sartori 1984).

The Cressey Catalyst

Much of the conceptual discrepancy that taints the study of organized crime can be traced to the 1969 publication of Cressey's *Theft of the Nation*. This book, produced after the author's participation in the 1967 President's Crime Commission in the United States, attracted an abundance of criticism and sparked a generation of work aimed at refuting its many claims.

---

1 Sartori (1984) maintains that collective ambiguity results from a trend towards either *homonymy* or *synonymy*. The former represents the popular usage of 'organized crime' and denotes a situation in which one word is assigned more than one meaning or 'a situation in which (at the limit) each scholar ascribes his own meanings to his key terms' (p. 35). The latter characterizes the scholarly context, where many words are used for the same meaning or referent. The ideal for any field of research is to arrive at a one-word, one-meaning concept.

Since the 1951 Kefauver Commission, a public inquiry had arisen over the emergence of a criminal society purposely put together to dominate and more efficiently organize the illegal distribution of goods and services in America. Cressey, a confessed sceptic concerning the existence of a nationwide organization of criminals, changed his opinion when confronted with the Commission's body of data, which led him to state that 'no rational man could read the evidence that I have read and still come to the conclusion that an organization variously called "the Mafia," "Cosa Nostra," and "the syndicate," does not exist' (1969: p. x). Unfortunately, he provided few details regarding his sources, aside from having relied primarily on various law enforcement and investigative materials (wire-tapping, other forms of electronic surveillance, interviews with 'knowledgeable policemen and investigators') as well as various informant testimonies.

Basing his study on such data, Cressey developed what would become the academic embodiment of the bureaucratic and nationwide conspiracy model of organized crime. The key findings and propositions from this argument are as follows: (1) that an exclusively Italian American nationwide criminal confederation and cartel, known as the Cosa Nostra, had been in existence since the early 1930s; (2) that the Cosa Nostra was rationally designed in a formal and hierarchical system that had the double role of governing body and cartel organizer; and (3) through means of force and corruption, the Cosa Nostra maintained a monopoly on the distribution of illegal goods and services in America and was penetrating an increasing number of legitimate industries.

Reaction against Cressey's work was immediate. Hawkins (1969) dismissed the validity of his claims as well as criticizing various arguments concerning membership, formal codes and sanctioning within such organizations, and the existence of a national conspiracy. Albini (1971) and Ianni (1972) pursued such criticisms and offered alternative interpretations centring on patron-client and kinship networks. Smith (1971) similarly confronted the organized crime vision offered by Cressey and was one of the first to direct attention away from the stereotypical term 'organized crime' and towards the notion of illegal enterprise.[2] Smith's reasoning was straightforward:

---

2 But see Sellin (1963) for an earlier use of this particular term.

The choice of a name other than 'organized crime' is a deliberate effort to escape from a concept so overburdened with stereotyped imagery that it cannot meet the basic requirements of a definition – it does not include all the phenomena that are relevant; it does not exclude all the phenomena that are not relevant. (p. 10)

Although Smith's assessment of the messy state of the notion of organized crime was accurate – then and now – the decision to create a new and independent term to resolve the matter was questionable. Like most others who took issue with Cressey's study, Smith disagreed not with the idea of organized crime per se but with Cressey's claim of the existence 'of a palpable cohesive, authoritarian, national structure' (Smith 1975: p. 21), referred to as the Cosa Nostra, and the way in which this questionable super-organization subsequently became the principal referent for the notion of organized crime. Indeed, this claim was at the centre of most criticisms of *Theft of the Nation* (Albini 1988; Haller 1992). A highlight in the evolution of this over-arching concept was the 1951 Kefauver hearings, which were the first to incorporate previously separate notions (e.g., gangster, racketeer, Mafia) under the general heading of organized crime and to assign, to any individual fitting such imageries, membership in the Mafia. The 1963 McClellan Commission introduced the testimony of Joe Valachi, an apparent Cosa Nostra soldier in New York City who became one of the first informants to supply law enforcement officials with such claims. The 1967 President's Commission, in turn, made such claims the driving force behind a substantial number of reforms that were outlined in the 1970 Organized Crime Control Act. Cressey, in the end, was the 'reputable sociologist' (Smith 1975: p. 307) who brought the perspective into social-scientific circles.

Explicit distinctions between that which was perceived as criminal enterprise and that which Cressey maintained was organized crime laid the direction for the crooked conceptual path that organized crime research thereafter took. Studies within the illegal enterprise alternative pointed out that what was for years perceived as organized crime did not necessarily conform to the rigid organizations put forward by Cressey. Such refutations grew into a conceptual distinction, which consequently led to an unwarranted referent split. Hence, if an activity or association of individuals was not formally organized, long term and monopolistic, totalitarian in its internal order, tightly knit, systematically violent and corrupt, and spanning a wide geographical plane, it was ipso facto not organized crime but illegal enterprise. However, critiques of Cressey's study and of the bureaucratic framework for which he became the principal exponent did overlook some key points raised in *Theft of the Nation*, points that would become the underpinnings of alternative theories and conceptual configurations.

For example, while most of Cressey's work described the tightly structured and dual governmental and business functions of the American Cosa Nostra, he also had much to say about a reorganizational trend that had been taking place and would persist in the years following his study. Cressey had explicitly predicted that the Cosa Nostra would gradually shift from a rank-ordered to a task-oriented entrepreneurial structure and would therefore likely decentralize. Expertise would replace loyalty within the organization. This expectation was largely neglected by his critics, who focused on the more sensationalist issues that the author defended, such as the national conspiracy claim. While the decentralization of the Cosa Nostra has yet to be documented, the issue of decentralization was upheld as a key contrast to Cressey's understanding of organized crime. In scholarly research, bureaucratic-like organized crime became organized crime, and illegal enterprise became the more decentralized alternative to organized crime.

This conceptual situation hampered the creation of more general theoretical frameworks and the search for cross-variant explanatory factors. Although I remain a curious reader of the considerable efforts that have been devoted to such conceptual concerns, my approach is almost exclusively analytical. The proposed framework avoids the conventional trap of falling into a single and stereotypical vision of organized crime as a criminal conspiracy that presents a massive public threat. It also avoids placing independent criminal entrepreneurs on an altogether different plane from organizational criminal entrepreneurs.[3]

Basic Assumptions and Orientation of the Proposed Framework

Achievement in entrepreneurial settings requires an ability to avoid obstacles and potential problems within a competitive arena. Achieve-

---

3 An elaborate and detailed historical analysis of both the social reaction and conceptual debate surrounding organized crime is offered by Woodiwiss (2001). The author's use of the term is quite wide: 'my understanding of the phrase "organized crime" is literal and short – organized crime is systematic criminal activity for money or power' (p. 3).

ment in criminal enterprise requires a similar ability. Although like legitimate enterprise in terms of cost-avoidance incentives, criminal practices are generally more pronounced in the extent and form of such costs. The consequences of product illegality put forward by Reuter (1983) in his seminal study of loan-sharking, numbers, and bookmaking markets in New York City during the 1970s tells us that participants in illegal markets are confronted with greater obstacles within the context of their business activities than their legitimate counterparts: (1) contracts are not enforceable by law; (2) participants are consistently at risk of having their assets seized at any time that they come under the scope of law enforcement targeting; and (3) participants face the risk of official sanctions, such as arrests or imprisonment (Reuter 1983: p. 114).

Using transaction-cost analysis, Reuter also revealed a key element concerning the informal nature of group structuring within illegal markets. Once again because of the consequences of product illegality, Reuter argued that in order to avoid the costs extending from participation in illegal markets, participants tend to come together in small and ephemeral groups in their business ventures (1983: p. 109). His central explanation for this finding points to the market forces confronting participants who are active in such groups. In shaping the structure of groups, such invisible-hand mechanisms were argued to prevail over those visible-hand forces (most notably violence) professed by advocates of the bureaucratic or orthodox perspective of organized crime in shaping the structure of groups. Reuter stated: 'it is not generally optimal for such a group to attempt to create monopolies within the underlying illegal markets. The organization of illegal markets is largely determined by economic forces' (p. 109). According to him, markets prevail over hierarchies in structuring the group efforts of participants.

Although Reuter's refutation of the bureaucratic perspective of organized crime serves as an important element in my argument, I question his positioning of the market as the dominant structuring force in illegal business settings. This disagreement is rooted in the fact that Reuter did not extend his analysis beyond activity-based group structures. As Tremblay (1993) emphasized, in rethinking a key aspect of Reiss' (1986, 1988) work on co-offending, an analysis of co-offending (or groups mobilized for crime) must account for not only event/activity-specific co-offending but the generally overlooked 'possibility that a given offender's crime career depends on the way it intersects or consciously parallels the crime sequences of various co-offenders' (p. 18).

While Reiss found that most offenders combine a mix of solo and group offending in their illicit activities, Tremblay stressed that this finding may be displaced by focusing on the availability of suitable co-offenders that increase (or, in the inverse trend, limit) the scope of opportunities offenders may take part in. In short, Reiss is concerned with what offenders do and with whom they do it, while Tremblay argues for an understanding of whom offenders know and what that allows them to do.

Tremblay's suggestion takes into consideration the choice-structuring properties put forward by Clarke and Cornish (1985) (see also Cornish and Clarke 1986), and emphasized by Akerstrom (1985) and Steffensmeier (1986), that '"finding" a suitable pool of partners, intermediaries, and contacts constitutes in fact a crucial, focal, problematic ... concern for a wide range of motivated potential offenders' (Tremblay 1993: p. 18). This approach converges on the criminal opportunities that extend from one's pool of available and suitable co-offenders. These opportunities allow for participation in specific criminal ventures or activities. Such junctures propagate throughout the development of a career in crime.

Understanding the structure of illegal market groupings, in this sense, calls for a focus not on how illegality changes the structure of groups that perform a specific task or mobilize for a short-term venture in a given illegal market, but on how illegal market and trade participants compensate for difficulties in sustaining working groups that are organized for long-term participation in criminal market settings. It is quite conceivable that all illegal market participants are limited by the consequences of product illegality and hence are restricted to groups mobilized for short-term projects. However, this does not entail that participants in such groups are limited to one short-term venture at a time. Participants may have short-term experiences in any of their group ventures, but, as individuals, their systematic access to such ephemeral groups makes their involvement in crime a long-term quest. Simultaneous and varied venturing allows a participant to further compensate for the risks associated with criminal business activities. So, while Reuter (1983) suggests that 'the most immediate consequence of product illegality ... is the need to control the flow of information about participation in the illegal activity ... so as to assure that the risk of exposure about participation is kept to a minimum' (p. 114), I argue that one way of avoiding this limitation in advancing a career in criminal enterprise is to structure the control of information in one's favour. This means that successful illegal market participants are those players who are in a position to control information so as to simultaneously assure their security and expand their personal access to opportunities that allow them to participate in a broader and overlapping range of activities. The focus, therefore, is not on one activity or market and how groups are structured therein, but on the participant's capacity to operate in a multitude of group ventures.

The present argument therefore departs from Reuter's invisible-hand thesis by focusing on the capacity of criminal entrepreneurs to successfully avoid the problems associated with participation in illegal markets. The extent to which an illegal market participant is active depends on his[4] access to others who serve as channels to available opportunities. Reuter (1983) was accurate in highlighting the informal nature of illegal market relations (as opposed to the formal structures put forward by the bureaucratic perspective of organized crime); however, it is also within the ensemble of these informal groupings that the main vehicle of action – the entrepreneur's personal network of working contacts – may also be found.

This study is less concerned with the motivations of criminal entrepreneurs. My primary interest is, quite differently, in what some criminal entrepreneurs have done and achieved throughout their careers. To echo Homans' (1961) success proposition, past achievement breeds further motivation. Yet, that all aspire to a life of outlaw freedom and materialistic comfort is one thing; that all achieve this on a long-term and successful basis is quite another.

For participants in criminal enterprise and long-term money-oriented criminal activities in general, tutelage and criminal forms of social capital are themselves key requirements for endurance and any level of achievement. Beyond capacity, participants share a common outlook. All have one common adversary: law enforcement officials and the conventional system that the law represents. This recalls Sutherland's assertion that 'regardless of how strong [is] the ill feeling between two thieves, neither of them would want to see the other pinched, and each would exert much effort to prevent it' (1937: p. 5). It also evokes Jack Black's personal observation that 'the masonry of the road and jungle would protect him against the common enemy – the

---

4 I use 'his' and 'he' throughout because most participants in illegal markets are male.

law' (2000: p. 165). Beating the conventional system of rules and formal control is taken as a collective incentive encouraging cooperation in illegal business settings.

While subcultural theories of crime have accentuated a cohesive normative setting that brings segments of the offender population together under the rubric of a similar way of life, this common-front outlook emphasizes collaboration amongst very different criminal participants who pool resources and transmit information in a process that extends from a collective incentive to beat the systemic odds facing them all. The main theoretical distinction is therefore between a normative/pull versus anarchic/rejection process that shapes working relations between outlaws.

2 A Personal Network Framework for Criminal Enterprise

How can one endure for two decades as an international cannabis smuggler without having the organizing force and support of a reputed and resource-yielding criminal organization? How, at the same time, may we account for the consistent findings throughout the past three decades that criminal organizations, such as the Mafia or Cosa Nostra (or any other ethnically defined criminal unity), are not structured along the formal criteria professed by Cressey (1969) and consistently maintained in official, law-enforcement accounts?[1] While past studies have generally turned to explanations in which the capacity and reputation for violence and corruption are regarded as the principal regulators of competition, the social network paradigm allows for the development of an alternative argument centred on relational utility.

Networks, Purposive Action, and the Emergence of Relational Asymmetry

Social network analysis has been on a sharp rise for over half a century as the framework of choice for social theorists and analysts alike. I will focus exclusively on a branch of it that has gained increasing attention throughout the past two decades or so.[2] This branch, which centrally

---

1 For criticisms of the official view, see Hawkins (1969); Albini (1971); Smith (1975); Anderson (1979); Haller (1990, 1991); Beare (1996); Naylor (1997); Hess (1998); Beare and Naylor (1999); Woodiwiss (2001); Sabetti (2002).
2 For extensive reviews of the social network paradigm as a whole, see Leinhardt (1977); Alba (1982); Wellman (1983); Scott (1991); Baker (1992); Wasserman and Faust (1994); Wellman and Berkowitz (1997); Watts (2003); and Freeman (2004). For more

employs the concept of social embeddedness or the relational structuring of purposive or instrumental action, emerges from the work of various economic sociologists or, in Granovetter's (1985) terms, within the intellectual spectrum of a 'new economic sociology' (see also Swedberg 1990).

How a network of contacts embeds individual actions has much to do in orienting the twists and turns that a given criminal career may take. The concept of social embeddedness is used to grasp the structuring force represented by social networks in curbing, ameliorating, and directing economic action. Such relational structuring of one's business ventures is crucial to 'generating trust and discouraging malfeasance' (Granovetter 1985: p. 490) between co-participants. The network, rather than the market or hierarchy, becomes the principal structure governing the economic actions of individuals:

> Actors do not behave or decide as atoms outside a social context, nor do they adhere slavishly to a script written for them by the particular intersection of social categories that they happen to occupy. Their attempts at purposive action are instead embedded in concrete, ongoing systems of social relations. (Granovetter 1985: p. 487)

Powell (1990) expands on this approach by discussing the advantages of network organizations in comparison to more traditional organizational systems:

> Networks are 'lighter on their feet' than hierarchies. In network modes of resource allocation, transactions occur neither through discrete exchanges nor by administrative fiat, but through networks of individuals engaged in reciprocal, preferential, mutually supportive actions. Networks can be complex: they involve neither the explicit criteria of the market, nor the familiar paternalism of the hierarchy. The basic assumption of network relationships is that one party is dependent on resources controlled by

---

exclusive theoretical and insightful concerns, see Collins (1988: Chapter 12); Haines (1988); Galaskiewicz and Wasserman (1993); Emirbayer and Goodwin (1994); and Emirbayer (1997). Methods and analytical techniques are presented and discussed quite thoroughly in Knoke and Kuklinski (1982); Marsden (1990); Scott (1991); and Wasserman and Faust (1994). For French overviews and methodological elaborations of network theory and applications, see Degenne and Forsé (1994) and Lemieux (1999).

another, and that there are gains to be had by the pooling of resources ...
Networks are particularly apt for circumstances in which there is need for
efficient, reliable information. The most useful information is rarely that
which flows down the formal chain of command in an organization, or
that which can be inferred from shifting price signals. Rather, it is that
which is obtained from someone whom you have dealt with in the past
and found to be reliable. You trust best information that comes from
someone you know well. (pp. 303–4)

Such advantages of the network over other forms of organization
have also been illustrated by Baker and Faulkner, who highlighted its
'flexible and self-adapting' qualities in business contexts (1993: p. 422).
More recent research has demonstrated that understanding the true
flow of information within business firms across a variety of industries calls less for an apprehension of the firm's formal structure and
internal ranking than for an elaborated effort to identify key and often
overlooked members within the firm that serve as strategic vectors
between others within and beyond the firm (see also Cross and Parker
2004).

Lin (1982), in his theory of instrumental actions, developed a representation of a pyramidal structuring of positioning in a given setting.
This pyramid structure is not designed along authoritarian forms of
control, but through differential access to resources. Individuals with
higher positions have a better vision over all other positions and are
therefore more likely to have better access and control of social resources within the organization. Social resources were defined, following Granovetter's earlier work on weak ties (1973, 1974, 1982) and later
formulation of social embeddedness (1985), as 'resources embedded in
one's social network' (Lin 1982: p. 132). Influence within such vertically
structured settings is differentially allocated in accordance with the
resources controlled by the participating actors and the privileges that
extend from such control. Higher-positioned participants (or participants with the most access to resources) gain an advantage over lower-
positioned participants because

any 'favor' the lower position may provide can be expected to have a
greater future payoff, since the higher position has more to offer the lower
position than vice versa. The information factor is associated with asymmetric network relations across levels of positions. A higher position
tends to have more information or a better view of the structure than a

lower position; thus, it is more capable of locating the specific resources embedded in the structure. (Lin 1982: p. 133)

Lin develops three propositions from this. First, 'the success of instrumental action is associated positively with the social resources provided by the contact' (p. 133). This is so because a better allocation of resources is more likely to help the actor reach his goal. Second, 'the level of the initial position is positively related to social resources reached through a contact' (p. 134). This is so because the initial position, whether inherited or acquired, situates the actor within reach of lateral and higher-level resources. Higher initial positioning therefore allows access to more valuable resources within the given setting. Third, 'weak ties rather than strong ties tend to lead to better resources' (p. 134). This last hypothesis arises directly out of Granovetter's (1973) weak-tie argument, which demonstrates the advantages goal-oriented actors (job searchers, in Granovetter's study) have in dealing with weakly linked contacts who do not share the same channels of information as the actor himself. Strongly linked contacts (i.e., family and close friends) are more likely to share the same knowledge and social resources as the actor, and are therefore less useful when seeking a goal that requires access to new forms of information. Weak ties are more beneficial when the actor is seeking something that is beyond his immediate reach. Access to new information increases one's standing amongst others. This creates the basis of relational asymmetry within networks built for competitive settings.

Structural Hole Theory

This overall conceptualization of the network vis-à-vis the market or hierarchy and as a structure with inherent asymmetries developed around differential access to resources (or opportunities) is consistent with the key theoretical and operational framework used throughout various segment of this study. Ron Burt's (1992) structural hole theory of competitive behaviour, which is the main influence for the framework under development, begins with an instrumental view of networks as a basis for social stratification:

> Society may be viewed as a market in which people exchange all variety of goods and ideas in pursuit of their interests. Certain people, or certain groups of people, do better in the sense of receiving higher returns to their

efforts. Some people enjoy higher incomes. Some more quickly become prominent. Some lead more important projects. The interests of some are better served than the interests of others. (Burt 2001: pp. 31–2)

Burt's theory is considerably influenced by Granovetter's weak ties and social embeddedness arguments, Lin's developments of the concept of instrumental vertical mobility in social networks, and, as Burt himself has stated, by Freeman's (1977) concept of between-ness centrality, Cook and Emerson's (1978) work on exchange networks, and Simmel's (1955) and Merton's (1957) ideas on conflicting social affiliations.[3] Rather than use markets or constraining hierarchy models in designing criminal entrepreneurs' scopes of action, the network model provides the main structural components that allow the observer to consider and gain insight into both risk-reducing and opportunity-expanding methods of increasing personal capacities. While this assumption is at the core of structural hole theory, it is also consistent with the ideas and theories arising from the purposive action approach within the social network paradigm. It leads to an additional assumption that centres on the concept of social capital:

> Social capital is the contextual complement to human capital. The social capital metaphor is that the people who do better are somehow better connected. Certain people or certain groups are connected to certain others, trusting certain others, obligated to support certain others, dependent on exchange with certain others. Holding a certain position in the structure of these exchanges can be an asset in its own right. That asset is social capital, in essence, a concept of location effects in differentiated markets. (Burt 2001: p. 32)

Structural hole theory tells us that having quicker access to information benefits in the competitive arena enables some players to fill positions that allow them to seize the more rewarding opportunities available (Burt 1992). This competitive edge extends from a player's capacity to effectively and efficiently enrich a personal network with a proportion-

---

3 Further influences on Burt's theory may be found in White's demonstrations of holes (vacancies leaving seizeable opportunities) in the network surrounding a person. (See White [1970] for vacancy chains, as well as White, Boorman, and Breiger [1976] and Boorman and White [1976] for blockmodelling designs extending from these earlier insights.)

ally higher set of entrepreneurial opportunities or *structural holes*. Because network ties, particularly in a business context, require time and energy to make and maintain, some contacts, in a sense, are better investments than others: 'What matters is the number of non-redundant contacts. Contacts are redundant to the extent that they lead to the same people, and so provide the same information benefits' (Burt 1992: p. 17). Hence, a participant (ego) is in a redundant relationship with alter A if alter A is in contact with most or all of ego's remaining alters. Redundant networking means that ego is investing his time and energy in closed and cliquish relational settings.

To be increasingly non-redundant, a participant must work at filling his personal network with the most structural holes possible. The structural hole is defined as 'an opportunity to broker the flow of information between people, and control the form of projects that bring together people from opposite sides of the hole' (Burt 1999: p. 6). These structural holes are therefore opportunities to broker between disconnected others. The competitive edge that some players may achieve over others comes from their heightened capacity to enrich their personal networks with entrepreneurial opportunities.

Such an insight is crucial not only, as Burt demonstrated, for understanding variations in success in legitimate enterprise settings, but also for embracing the achievement continuum in criminal enterprise. It allows us to see that the central players that are typically targeted and receive the most attention are not necessarily the most prosperous players within a given illicit market, venture, or organization. Instead, it promotes the idea that the most prosperous players are positioned on the peripheries of such spheres of action. These are the brokers of information between the more visible players. They are the most insulated yet strategically positioned to participate consistently and for a longer duration in a wider range of ventures.

Some players have the freedom to choose to develop the network benefits of information, and may therefore come to control other competitors to a certain degree. Some players with such freedom will choose to further cultivate that capacity, and others not. Another group of players in the competitive arena does not have access to such opportunities; they therefore do not have any choice but to seek out and depend on the social capital of others.

Burt's theory and the purposive network perspective from which it arises are key to the advancement of criminal enterprise research as well as more general research in criminology. They respond to Agnew's (1995) assessment that few criminologists have discussed the factors that promote freedom of choice, although it has been argued that free choice is most likely when there is an absence of constraint or there are countervailing constraints, and when the individual has the drive and the capacity to engage in self-directed behaviour. (p. 88)

Burt (1992) offers the analytical framework that allows us to incorporate the concepts of choice, constraint, and self-directed behaviour. A crime-oriented model guided by such precepts therefore shifts from soft determinism when converging on the early stage of a criminal career – a stage that is decisive in guiding the direction of the actor's drift, in Matza's (1964) sense – into an indeterminist position once entry into a milieu is achieved and commitment to a criminal career is substantially established. Upon entry and commitment, 'actors have the freedom of action and freedom of choice on at least some occasions' (Agnew 1995: p. 89). The level of such occasions increases with one's capacity. Capacity is a precursor to both forms of freedom, and although full freedom (complete autonomy) may never be achieved, the likelihood of extensive survival and increasing freedom within an illegal trade is shaped by a player's ability to further the interests of others in that milieu and to shape those interests in his favour. The approach is determinist because others play key roles in deciding what you can do. It is indeterminist because you can control how others are able to control you.

Four measures are offered to apply structural hole theory. Each captures a unique dimension of non-redundant networking. The most straightforward and the base of all other measures is *effective size*, which computes the difference between the number of contacts and the sum of the proportions of dyadic redundancy that each contact maintains within a given player's network (call this player 'ego'). If a given contact is in full-strength relationship (coded 100) with all other contacts, his dyadic redundancy is $(n-1)/n$ (where n is the number of ego's contacts). Hence, perfect clique networks, in which all contacts are connected to each other with equal strength, yield a minimum effective size of 1.[4] In such a network, all contacts are redundant and ego is investing all his

---

4 For example, ego reports having three especially close (100) contacts that are all interconnected at full strength (100). The dyadic redundancy, $(n-1)/n$, for each contact is 0.666... (2/3). The effective size for ego's network is obtained by subtracting the sum of the proportions of dyadic redundancy (0.666 × 3) from the overall number of contacts (hence, 3 − 2 = 1).

relational time and energy in a single unit (the clique). At the other extreme is the perfect broker network, in which ego serves as the sole connector between all contacts (with relationships between all contacts having a 0 value). In such dispersed networks, a maximum effective size equals the number of contacts in the personal network (all contacts are non-redundant).[5] A useful way of expressing such a network property is to calculate the ratio between effective size and the total number of contacts within the network. This is referred to as *network efficiency* and, in its simplest form, represents the proportion of contact disconnectivity in a personal network. Our clique member displays minimal network efficiency for a three-contact network at 33 per cent (effective size = 1/total contacts = 3). Inversely, our broker displays maximum network efficiency at 100 per cent (3/3).

A more elaborate structural hole measure that builds on the effective size measure is *network constraint* or, inversely (1 – constraint), network autonomy. In its most candid form, constraint indicates the 'knots' within a personal network. It incorporates the extent to which ego invests in a particular contact before assessing to what degree that contact overlaps with others in ego's network. As in the knot analogy, it measures the extent to which the network around a person is closed (Coleman 1988) in the sense that everyone around the person is connected either directly or indirectly through a few key people. Building bridges across structural holes to other groups decreases network constraint. High constraint indicates a person with few degrees of freedom (low autonomy) in his or her relationships.

How free are organized crime participants to expand such network-based opportunities? Reuter's (1983) discussion of the consequences of product illegality, Erickson's (1981) work on secret societies, and Baker and Faulkner's (1993) findings regarding price-fixing schemes suggest that constraint-free networking in criminal and clandestine contexts remains far from given. Because of threats posed by exposure of one's illegal activities, the risks of expansion are numerous and career damaging and, as a result, participants in prolonged illegal activities prefer to invest in security over efficiency in their working methods.

Constraint is an indication that a criminal entrepreneur is at the building (or rebuilding) stage of his career. It suggests that he is in a

---

5 In this example, another ego also reports having three especially close (100) contacts that are all disconnected (0) from each other. Ego's effective size is the overall number of contacts – the sum of the proportions of dyadic redundancy, and hence, 3 – 0 = 3.

relatively low opportunity context, and it is expected to decrease as his career ascends. Constraint in criminal networks indicates the level of relationally situated risk that ego is facing at any given time. The higher the constraint in ego's network, the higher the likelihood that ego is compelled to seize opportunities that he himself must seek out.

More entrepreneurial (less constrained) personal networks permit ego to increase, broaden, and vary his activities by participating in or simultaneously brokering between more clusters of co-participants. Accessing information from such an improved entrepreneurial position allows ego to be the vector of more information and to control benefits. As a broker within a bounded network, he receives information about various resources that is subsequently transmitted to others within the network. Brokers (highly efficient or low-constrained entrepreneurs) are well positioned to receive quicker, more recent, and better information-based opportunities within a wider and more dispersed network of contacts. Who receives the information once it reaches the broker is the decisive privilege of that broker. Indeed, more than one broker may exist within the same bounded working setting, but the position is fitting for only a specific few.

The inverse case occurs, once again, for ego who is situated in a clique. Because time and energy are allocated equally amongst contacts, ego cannot benefit from the additional resources and opportunities he would access if investing exclusively in one contact within the clique. This latter strategy would allow ego to increase the returns on his relational investment because, rather than spending X time and energy with Y contacts, he would spend $1/X$ time and energy on $1/Y$ of the contacts (call this one contact 'A'). He would still have indirect access to and therefore make use of the $Y - 1$ contacts because he would remain in contact with A, who remains connected to others in the clique. This is not only efficient and low-constrained networking, but it is also crucial for long-term criminal action in that it permits ego to reduce his exposure to others.

Structural hole measures are indicative of both ego's opportunities and his exposure within a clandestine working environment and to external targeting forces. Efficiency or low personal network constraint suggests high opportunities and lower risk. Low constraint indicates higher risk because ego is interacting with others who are not as tightly linked within his personal network. In terms of trust and security, Burt (2001) argues that high constraint is less risky than low constraint. It is true that trust and security are more likely established amongst strongly linked contacts. But it is also true, as game theorists would point out, that your most trusting contact is also in the best position to impede your security (Axelrod 1984). Taking this dilemma into consideration, we might therefore maintain that although Burt's argument regarding constraint and security does make sense, low constraint offers a less risky working network for players who are trying to diminish the probability of personal detection, because they are generally playing in the buffer zone or within the holes in their network. High constraint, in turn, suggests dependence on others within the working network, pointing to access to opportunities controlled by others and higher operational visibility.

Because constraint is a likely obstacle during the building phase of a criminal entrepreneurial career, a striving ego is best suited to become *hierarchically constrained*. This fourth measure highlights a networking strategy that has ego concentrating his constraints in one or a small set of established alters. This should be especially the case for organizationally confined criminal entrepreneurs who emerge from relatively closed working settings. Burt (1992, 1998), in studying legitimate members of organizations, found that certain members of a firm (women and entry-level men who were regarded as outsiders or illegitimate members of the firm) who are intent on getting ahead are obliged to invest their relational time and energy in a more strategic fashion in order to make the most of their inevitably low-opportunity positions: 'key for outsiders breaking into the game is to borrow social capital rather than build it. Legitimate [accepted and established] members of a population succeed by building their own social capital. Illegitimate members of the population have to borrow' (1998: p. 6). Borrowing a legitimate or established member's social capital puts one in a hierarchically constrained relation with that strategic sponsor. In this sense, ego is structuring his network to have one or two large knots rather than many small ones.

In shaping personal network constraints via a hierarchical strategy, ego is able to increase his personal exposure with the assurance of a sponsor who serves as a screening and vouching device between ego and other players within the sponsor's network. The sponsor is essentially brokering between ego and others. Indirect access to such an entrepreneurial player's network may be beneficial to those who are at the building phase of their careers; however, such a personal network design also keeps ego dependent on the sponsor.

Once ego becomes accepted as a trusted insider within the firm and is able to have direct business relations with the sponsor's contacts, he must branch out on his own at some point. If he does so by decreasing the hierarchical dependency he has on the sponsor and expanding his network to be more entrepreneurial, he is then an organizational member whose career is ascending. Within the firm, this may result in earlier, faster, and more promotions. Within business activities, ego is expected to increase returns on his investment of relational time and energy because he is able to spread his resources more efficiently and decrease his risks across a better and autonomous selection of network-based opportunities.

Those participants in the criminal market or trade who attain such a non-redundantly characterized and entrepreneurially fit brokerage position place themselves so that they control not others, but the information and resources that others need. The criminal entrepreneur operating within a non-redundant relational context is more capable of adapting to crisis throughout his career. This is so because he is more 'robust' in his actions (Padgett and Ansell, 1993) and in a more suitable position to adapt to incoming events and life sequences that are beyond his full control. He is, in short, more flexible in the working environment that surrounds his earning activities. Criminal careers that reach successful heights are therefore expected to proceed through various movements that are relationally structured. The transitions that take a person from increasing efficiency in investing time and energy in others, decreasing constraint, and, if necessary, an abandoning of hierarchical dependency carry that person towards structural autonomy and privilege within the competitive arena.

This network-oriented edge offers an alternative mechanism for studying variations in capacities for crime, as well as for accounting for divergence in outcomes. It allows us to evaluate competition for positions in illegal business settings through the informal forces that are systematically at work in both criminal or legitimate settings. The major distinction between criminal and legitimate business settings, aside from the obvious prohibition applied to the former, is that criminal milieus cannot be feasibly set in any formal structure. The informal processes that come forward are best revealed when set within the context of network structures that are conducive in both criminal and legitimate spheres. Such relationally based insights may not have been explicitly formulated in past research on organized and other forms of money-oriented crime, but they have been consistently present on an implicit level.

Entrepreneurial Behaviour in Illegal Trades: Insights on Criminal Networks

Past research on organized crime and criminal market settings has left us with a series of snapshots that have yet to be gathered within a common theoretical framework. The remainder of this chapter raises a series of issues concerning the cooperative and informal nature of competition in activities associated with criminal enterprise and the inner working relations that allow some participants to get ahead of others.

Informal and Interest-Based Cooperation

Careers in criminal enterprise are competitive processes built on cooperative capacities. Reuter and Haaga (1989) conducted interviews with forty importers, wholesalers, and retailers incarcerated in American federal prisons. Their study revealed two findings that remain of interest here. First, they found that 'capital in this business consists almost entirely of an inventory which is turned over very rapidly and the "good will" built up by knowing good suppliers and customers' (p. 35). Second, 'successful operation does not require creation of a large or enduring organization' (p. 54). Although formal organizations may have existed, they were not prerequisites for operational or financial success in the trade; hence, 'trading relationships ... were more like networks than like hierarchical organizations' (p. 54). Participants were perceived more as 'independent salesmen' dealing in non-exclusive and decentralized 'arms-length-buyer-seller relations' (p. 44; see also Naylor [1997] for a similar insight). Furthermore, the authors surmised that 'the whole structure of the trades is based on asymmetries of information that would preclude formal organization' (p. 46). Informal cooperation, rather than formal organization, was therefore deemed a more suitable notion in describing the collective nature of participation in drug importing.

   Potter (1994) also stressed the cooperative nature of interaction between organized crime groups. He showed, in his analysis of three main crime groups involved in illegal gambling operations, prostitution, drug trafficking, and counterfeiting in an undisclosed city in the United States, that the process of organized crime resembled that of any community-based social exchange network:

> Organized crime relations often tend to be informal, changing, and pre-
> dicted upon need and opportunity ... At the very least, organized crime
> represents a social network, a loose interplay of relationships among indi-
> viduals in the community who come together to pursue a goal. (p. 123)

Such an exchange system is also at the base of patron-client models of
organized crime that relate directly to the supply-demand of social
resources developed in the purposive network perspective introduced
earlier. Cooperation, in such frameworks, is again established with
business incentives at the forefront. Common goals are constituted in
each transactor's satisfaction with his receiving part in the exchange.
Such mutual exchange processes combine to create, as Reuter and
Haaga (1989) noted in the case of drug importers, asymmetries in the
overall network of overlapping transactors.

Patron-Client Networks

The idea of patron-client networks in criminal settings has its roots with
Albini (1971). In his study of 'syndicated crime' in the United States and
his critique of the Cressey-based formal organizational model of the
Cosa Nostra, he stressed the informal nature of criminal organizations
and described them 'in terms of a system of power relationships among
its participants' (p. 263). Albini maintained that formal titles associated
with organizational membership were 'not useful since, contrary to the
assumption of those who argue formal structure, not all bosses,
underbosses, lieutenants, or soldiers are equal in power or status'
(p. 264). Formal roles or titles[6] were perceived as minimal indicators of
a participant's influence in a given setting when contrasted with 'syndicated criminals who have managed to assume strong positions in power,
not in a formal structure, but because they are in positions to serve as
patrons to a syndicate criminal clientele' (p. 265). This suggests that a
participant's title and position amongst others who are active in the
same settings cannot be fully understood unless an in-depth analysis of
that person's influence amongst such others is assessed and revealed. A
pecking order is constructed around the informal give-and-take (pa-
tron-and-client) process that develops over time. The categories of patron or client positions, however, are not mutually exclusive in that
every patron can be a client of someone else:

---

6 Note that Albini (1971) does not deny the existence of formal titles within the syndicated crime under analysis.

> Powerful syndicate figures who serve as patrons to their functionaries may also serve as clients to others more powerful than they. Others may serve on an equal basis in that although they are both patrons having a large number of clients, they may exchange mutual services. (p. 265)

Albini's findings had an important impact on research that followed. For example, Ianni (1972), in his first-hand ethnographic study of the structure of an organized crime family (the Lupollos) across three generations, also found the exchange process to be a more accurate representation of the Cosa Nostra than the formal organizational aspects of more authoritarian-based explanations:

> The base of *Mafia* power is personal relationship ... Where the law is powerless, say the *mafioso*, the injured must have a recourse to his own strength and that of his friends. Such relationships are not based on functional requisites but on personal connections and relationships. The dependence on influence describes the exchange relationships of *mafia* which finds its persistence in the pattern of obligations and responsibilities established throughout favors and services. (p. 40)

Ianni supports the 'canon of reciprocity' (p. 148) when accounting for the main mechanisms and motives keeping members of a crime family and other affiliates in cooperative relations. However, because he stressed kinship or clan links in elaborating such relations, his study of the Italian American crime family (1972), like his later work on African American and Puerto Rican crime groups (1974), came to centre on the ethnic concentration of cooperative relations.

Few studies have remained consistent with this ethnic condition for cooperation in criminal enterprise. For example, McIllwain (2004) revisits New York City's Chinatown and its gambling, prostitution, and opium markets at the turn of the twentieth century. Although he does persist with the notion of 'Chinese organized crime,' his revisionist approach dismisses the claim to racial homogeneity. Whether within the studied vice markets or in assessing underworld-upperworld relations, McIllwain identifies the multi-ethnic mix that served as a basis for criminal networks that developed to seize the opportunities emerging from the larger political-economic system of which Chinatown activities were a part. McIllwain turns to Block (1983) in arguing that the social system uniting professional criminals, politicians, and clients in reciprocal services should be at the forefront when studying the organized criminal activities of specific groups or in particular regions. Such a social system was also at the centre of Chambliss's (1977) assessment of organized crime and corruption in Seattle. This social system can be expressed within a social network framework (see also McIllwain 1999).

Those who do report findings revealing ethnic homogeneity generally focus on an ethnically defined organized crime group to begin with (as would be the case with McIllwain's [2004] expression 'Chinese organized crime'). A network analysis takes us beyond the scope of analysis bounded by ethnic orientation. For some, however, it may well be that ethnic similarities are not a condition but a precursor extending from the social surroundings in which the personal networks of participants develop and overlap. Ethnic homogeneity, like gender concentration and other attributes, is more likely an indication of the social basin of the network than a requirement for the realization of relations and extended business ventures. Criminal networks may develop within the ethnically concentrated social contexts, but ethnic concentration is not, in any way, a condition for networks to develop.

Later studies of particular 'families' were able to identify the basis of structure without raising kinship issues. For example, Haller (1991), in his study of Philadelphia's Bruno family, related the group to a 'fraternal organization' that offered prestige, reputation, insulation, useful contacts, business opportunities, economic advantages, and a setting for the mutual exchange of favours between its members (p. 1). Haller described the reciprocal system in place under the leadership of Angelo Bruno for twenty-one years and that ended with his murder in 1980:

> Members and associates recognized they were part of a larger network of legal and illegal businessmen who were expected to do favors for each other, avoid acts of unfair competition, and not cheat those who ran businesses that were 'connected' to other members. (p. 17)

This cooperative working environment was considerably modified, argued Haller, once Bruno's successor (Nicky Scarfo) began advocating and using more violence and, through his 'self-interested policies,' weakened the 'group loyalty' (p. 24) that was in place throughout the Bruno years. 'Scarfo,' explains Haller, 'seized power within a family that had traditionally been a coalition of independent money-makers involved in a range of legal and illegal operations' (p. 24). Through his less cooperative policies, Scarfo fell prey to law enforcement tactics shortly after taking hold of the Philadelphia family when members and associates, who disapproved of and feared the increased level of instrumental violence and despotic tactics, began to cooperate with law enforcement officials as government witnesses.

Cooperative relations are indeed at the root of criminal enterprise. A lack of them would mean a short-lived existence for any form of clandestine transactional setting. Probably one of the more straightforward attempts to develop the image of the network-based model is Hess's (1998) study of the Sicilian Mafia. Hess focused on the nature of relationships within family (or *cosca*) unities and between mafiosi:

> The *cosca* is not a group; interaction and an awareness of 'we,' a consciousness of an objective to be jointly striven for, are absent or slight. Essentially it is a multitude of dyadic relationships maintained by the *mafioso* (m) with persons independent of each other (X ... Xn). Instead of being a single person, X can also represent a small group, usually a family; in other words, via X, m reaches one or more further persons along a chain of dyadic relationships ... This does not mean that X_1 and X_n do not know one another. On the contrary, they usually know very well who the other person is and in what relationship he stands to m, but it is only the *mafioso* who mobilises them for joint action. (pp. 80–1)

Hess's conceptualization of the structure of the *cosca* and the mafioso's place within reveals the brokerage-like quality of relationships in such settings. He further elaborated on this structure and revealed how dyadic reciprocal relationships generally become asymmetrical and transform into the patron-client relationships identified by Albini (1971):

> X is almost invariably the weaker partner; he is not [only] on a lower level economically and socially, but also in the power hierarchy. He therefore tends to regard m as his patron; similarly it is natural for m to treat X not as a partner but as a man dependent on him. This asymmetry becomes the more marked the longer a relationship lasts. (Hess 1998: pp. 82–3)

Although past research largely disregarded formal organizational structuring, it nevertheless emphasized inequality between co-participants. Competitive advantages in the patron-client model and other frameworks put forward to study organized crime are achieved through prolonged exchange processes between participants that, over time, remain reciprocal but become unbalanced in regard to what each par-

ticipant is receiving and to what degree one participant becomes systematically dependent on the other for future dealings. This is the core
of the power-based structure that is at the centre of this phenomenon
and that, in its general framework, concurs completely with the insights
provided by those purposive network theorists discussed earlier and,
particularly, the brokerage model put forward in Burt's (1992) structural hole argument.

Resource Pooling and Prolonged Scamming

Once in cooperation, co-transactors in a given venture have a considerable collective interest in keeping a 'good thing' going. This good thing
is not simply the potential financial yield of such continuous cooperation and resource mobilization, but the opportunity to repeatedly cooperate within the boundaries and relative security of trusted and
network-worthy contacts. There are some available enhancements
to this line of inquiry. Haller's (1990) work, in discussing 'criminal
partnerships,' coincides directly with Powell's (1990) network conceptualization provided earlier:

> A partnership model posits that each enterprise is a separate enterprise
> that pools resources and provides local management. ... Reliability as a
> partner (or, at least, the appearance of reliability) is important for career
> success. Smart entrepreneurs fulfill their obligations in order to be offered
> future opportunities ... Successful early cooperation [is] the key to more
> lucrative opportunities in subsequent years. (p. 222)

Illegal trade participants must be able to overcome the consequences
of product illegality and particularly the risk of detection by law enforcement. Haller accentuates the need for participants to remain proactive and flexible in their activities. Structural hole theory tells us that
for this to be possible, the participants must have access to an efficient
network of working contacts. The ability to raise capital and mobilize
a venture is therefore a function of a participant's extended pool of
contacts.

Block and Chambliss's (1981) study, as well as Block's (1979) article
on the cocaine trade in New York circa 1910–17, like Adler's (1993)
ethnography of cocaine and marijuana smugglers in the southwestern
United States, stressed the decentralized structure of illegal drug trafficking. The shape of business-oriented cooperation, consistent with the

groups usually identified in other trades built around the supply of illegal goods and services, was found to be 'fragmented,' 'kaleido-scop[ic],' and 'sprawling' (Block and Chambliss 1981: p. 56). Somewhat differently, Adler revealed the deviant business and social subculture within which smugglers were clustered to insulate themselves from the potential outgrowths of their illicit trafficking activities (Adler 1993).

Block and Chambliss (1981) explained the transitory and opportunistic nature of trade combinations:

> Their informal structures and probably short life spans were exceptionally responsive to the necessities of the drug trade. First of all, entry into the trade was fairly simple, involving few costs beyond the initial capital investment, few contacts in the area of supply, and hardly any organization for distribution ... It would be foolish to stake one's criminal career around a particular combination, given the chances that there would be nothing to sell ... It demanded entrepreneurs who were flexible, who had numerous contacts, and who were able to raise capital at unexpected times and to pull together a small organization with little effort. (p. 56)

As for future commitments not implemented in ongoing criminal ventures, it may well be that two individuals interacting for the first time in an illegal transaction will never see each other after that particular event, but Reuter and Haaga (1989) did maintain that the interests of suppliers and customers (at various intersections along the distribution chain) 'were held together by considerations of long-term mutual benefit; neither side would press its advantage in negotiating a single transaction to the point where the long-term relationship was destroyed' (p. 48).

The more general scenario would therefore have crime participants who are motivated to stay in contact with each other and maintain relations. In this sense, future commitments are not obligatory, but a good contact, marked by reliability, trustworthiness, and a capacity to offer consistent access to new or stable opportunities, is a contact that must be retained. Since one cannot realistically trust everyone, those who have established themselves as reliable and trustworthy are usually those with whom subsequent transactions will be made.

The limited selection of accomplices and partners in crime means that criminal opportunities for action are embedded within the realms of personal networks of family, friends, and acquaintances. The contacts of one's direct contacts (Boissevain's [1974] 'friends of friends') also supply a latent pool of co-participants. Finckenauer and Waring (1998) concluded along similar lines in their network study of the crimes of Russian immigrants in the Tri-State region of the United States (New York, New Jersey, and Pennsylvania) during the 1990s. They rejected claims of a 'Russian Mafia' dominance within that region, instead finding and focusing on the 'broad connectivity among most of the actors' (p. 198) who were included in the various sociograms offered in their study:

> [These actors] may not be directly connected to a large number of others, but they are indirectly connected to many. This allows the networks a great deal of flexibility in the organization of their offenses, which means they can be responsive to the opportunities for illegal undertakings that develop. Given such an opportunity, a member of these large networks can access partners who are either generalists or specialists, can raise capital, and can access other needed resources. (p. 198)

The social network represents the foundation from which outlaw partnerships, criminal ventures, and criminal enterprise extend and continue. Relational positioning within this interest-based exchange network of potential co-participants should therefore be the focus of analysis. Such relational positioning is marked by an actor's ability to be entrepreneurially flexible, and this entrepreneurial flexibility is indicated by the capacity to control the resources needed by others or, in other words, to place oneself within the interests of others. Simultaneous operating also comes with one's ability to acquire a place between the interests of others. Positioning oneself on the efficient side of the resource asymmetry makes one attractive to others who are seeking to supplement and shelter their own actions by accessing better quality information benefits. The case studies I offer in Chapters 4 and 5 build on these insights. Networks have always been fundamental to criminal enterprise; the task now is to focus directly on this relational aspect.

3 Sources and Method

Criminal Memoirs

The source that became the factual basis for the present study sprang to my attention not during a formalized and elaborately planned field-work project, but in a casual encounter. When she learned that I was researching drug trafficking networks, a Scottish optometrist I had met while travelling in Spain suggested I read the autobiography of Howard Marks (1997), a famous Welsh cannabis smuggler. After returning from Spain, I purchased Marks' book, *Mr. Nice*, and found it to be rich in details of the author's operations as an international cannabis trafficker, as well as revealing a wide array of contacts who were implicated in his activities throughout his lengthy career.

I passed the autobiography on to my PhD adviser at that time, Pierre Tremblay. After reading it, Pierre, ever insightful, suggested that I conduct an analysis and write a paper using the network approach I had been studying for the previous two years, with Marks' account as the main data source. The final product of this suggestion appears in the first of this book's case studies (see Chapter 4).

That this initial project yielded an interesting product (and mainly that the project came to an end) convinced me that the criminal memoir was an overlooked source and potential informational gold mine within direct reach. I began scanning through other biographies and autobiographies of organized crime figures, illegal market participants, and other career outlaws. Some accounts, of course, were superior to others, but most had the details that researchers seek when attempting to construct an empirical world. What was common across all the biographical accounts was the place of others in the central character's life. These key others that help shape and guide the events and transitions throughout a person's career are explicitly mentioned in the criminal memoir, with this relational foundation often serving as the story line. The names that emerge from these personal accounts represent an important portion of the central character's personal network.

In pursuing this idea of relational foundation, I became more selective in the case study that would follow Marks and replicate my developing approach. Eventually, I came across Maas' (1997) biography of Sammy (the Bull) Gravano. Gravano was a member of New York City's Gambino family who defected from that way of life after accepting a deal from the FBI that substantially diminished his expected sentence in return for his testimony against his Gambino boss, John Gotti, and other members of New York City's Cosa Nostra. His account further supported my view of the network basis of a career in crime. This result was largely expected, but I was also struck by a difference between these two criminal memoirs. While Marks was typical of the independent organized crime participant, Gravano's career had all the hallmarks of the tight organizational working structure that has been traditionally associated with Cressey's (1969) outline of the American Cosa Nostra and has become the target of a multitude of scholarly criticisms since. Yet this formal structuring, so apparent in Gravano's experience, was not in itself enough to constitute the network patterns at work throughout his career. The most revealing insight that emerged from each of these criminal career histories was how similar they were in their reliance on and use of others throughout their trajectories. The scheme was now in place. The study would incorporate a comparative approach that would focus on the structure and influences of the career personal networks of two diametrically opposed criminal entrepreneurs: the independent Marks and the organization-based Gravano.

Primary and Supplementary Data Sources for the Marks Case Study

Marks wrote his autobiography after his release from Terre Haute maximum security penitentiary in 1995. In an interview with a British newspaper shortly after the publication of *Mr. Nice*, the author was asked to describe the challenge of writing his life story. His answer provides some indication of the accuracy of this principal source: 'Writing the book was easy in one way because my life was so heavily documented by the American government that all I had to do was read Drug Enforcement Agency Observation Records to find out where I was at a particular time' (*Evening Herald*, 6 September 1996).

The principal venues for supplementary sources were an earlier journalistic account of the experiences of Marks' main Drug Enforcement Agency (DEA) nemesis during the latter half of the 1980s (see Eddy and Walden 1991) and a less personalized biography (Leigh 1988). I also consulted Marks' personal Web page,[1] which yielded two sources that permitted several cannabis trade ventures to be confirmed. Newspaper clippings from the 1980s are available and provide media confirmation of Marks' and his co-participants' larger drug-busts and judicial encounters. Confirmation of activities that took place throughout the 1970s was unattainable (aside from the ensemble of newspaper clippings included within the autobiography); however, the scope of activities throughout this earlier period proved consistently more restricted[2] than within later, more ambitious periods. Marks also provides his web-page visitors with access to some of the DEA electronic surveillance recordings from the first half of 1986 that were used in building a case against him, recordings in which he and his co-participants are engaged in the largest operations of his career. Confirmation (newspaper clippings and electronic surveillance) was retrievable for the largest consignments, less so for the more standard one-ton shipments. Finally, while the intercepted telephone conversations linked Marks with many of the people and events documented throughout his autobiography, several new, undocumented names appeared as well. These latter names were excluded from the set of possible contacts because of their absence from the principal data source.

Primary and Supplementary Data Sources for the Gravano Case Study

Maas' (1997) biography of Gravano, which was written in collaboration with the central character, served as a main source throughout this study, supplemented by various biographical, journalistic, law enforcement, prosecutorial, and academic sources. Among the latter was a biography of one of Gravano's key contacts at the height of his career, John Gotti (Capeci and Mustain 1996). This source proved useful in further elaborating Gravano's career, particularly throughout the 1980s. Because Gotti and Gravano worked in close proximity and came to share a common relational entourage, an account of the former's career provided considerable overlapping evidence for the latter's.

---

1 Marks' web page is located at www.mrnice.co.uk.
2 None of the importation shipments of cannabis documented from the 1970s surpassed one ton, the amount that Adler found to be standard for marijuana smuggling during the same period (1993: p. 56).

An additional biographical source that provided similarly confirming evidence focused on the Gambino family as a whole (Davis 1993). A third supplementary source extended from the sensationalist attention surrounding Gravano's defection from the Cosa Nostra and Gotti's subsequent conviction (Blumenthal and Miller 1992).[3] Electronic surveillance was the key law enforcement tactic used by the FBI in their targeting of various Gambino family members during the 1980s. A great deal of public interest surrounded the prosecution of Gotti, enough that the electronic-surveillance-based evidence as well as an edited version of Gravano's personal testimony (direct and cross-examination) used throughout the trial could profitably be published for mass market consumption.

Another law enforcement source was retrieved on the Internet. Between November 1991 and February 1992 (immediately following his defection from the Cosa Nostra to the FBI), Gravano went through a series of debriefings by the FBI. The contents of fifty-one of these debriefings can be downloaded at the Smoking Gun website.[4]

Additional supplementary sources confirmed a large part of Gravano's activities, particularly for his most prominent period during the 1980s. Three studies provided material on racketeering in New York City's construction industry (Jacobs 1994, 1999; Goldstock et al., 1990), Gravano's main business activity from the late 1970s to his 1990 arrest. These studies helped situate and further specify Gravano's contacts and venturing within that particular industry. As with the Marks case study, selection of contacts was limited to those documented in the primary biographical source (Maas 1997). Supplementary sources were used only to confirm or provide additional information regarding those contacts already selected.

Marks' autobiography and Maas' biography of Gravano are but two documents in a mass of other potential case study sources. Although such documents have often been dismissed for their spontaneous reporting style, anecdotal story-telling, and subjective view of various facets of crime, past research has nevertheless turned to published criminal auto/biographies as main or complementary factual sources (Sutherland 1937; Klockars 1974; Arlacchi 1983; Steffensmeier 1986; Katz 1988; Gambetta 1993; Firestone 1993; Shover 1996; Jacobs 1999). The criminal memoir has the benefit of offering an insider's vision within an offender's life trajectory. For my purposes, two sets of infor-

---

3 I thank New York City journalist Jerry Capeci for bringing this source to my attention.
4 http://www.thesmokinggun.com/gravano/gravano.html.

mation were particularly sought within each biographical source: (1) information on contacts or co-participants in crime, and (2) information on earning (illegal or legitimate) activities and career-relevant events.

That the criminal memoir lends itself to a network analytical strategy is not simply a coincidence. These life histories provide a wide array of research opportunities for studying the makings of criminal networks. One of the most striking characteristics readily evident to any reader of such literature is the consistent relational flow that serves as the backbone for many of these accounts. This is the egocentric-network structure of many criminal memoirs. The chronology of a participant's evolution from his entry into a given illegal activity, gradual rise and establishment of reputation, and eventual fall[5] generally takes place within a contact-to-contact narrative pattern. Associating major events and turning points throughout one's career with a name or group of names is common practice among writers of such accounts. The resulting documents are therefore valuable in identifying various transitions, events, or outcomes and determining the participants implicated in and around each. Although we cannot reasonably expect an author to report every contact that emerged throughout his criminal experience, such a source gives us access to at least the core personal network of the central character.

Developing the Method

The analytical segment of this study developed in two phases. First, the main analytical strategy and representations were created during an inductive analysis of Marks' career. Although the social network perspective was a mainstay from the onset, the relevance of Burt's structural hole theory within this study emerged only once the network and event aspects of Marks' career were extracted and organized. Burt's theory, in brief, provided the right fit. Once that case study was completed, the same representations were replicated within the context of Gravano's career, albeit with various modifications that accounted for some of the key differences between the two criminal entrepreneurs.

---

5 I include the fall among the general phases of the criminal auto/biographical account with a reasonable level of certainty. While not all criminal participants are expected to experience a career fall, its degree of probability among those who have had their stories published, many of them informants to begin with, is clearly much higher.

Identifying Outcomes

The first step in this method required a selection of contacts that were relevant to the criminal activities and events each criminal entrepreneur took part in throughout his career. For both case studies, the core working network was extracted from each account through a contact elimination strategy. As already noted, only principal sources (Marks 1997 and Maas 1997) were used in establishing the overall pool of contacts that served as the starting network sample. Supplementary sources helped in providing further information regarding contacts, but not in adding new contacts to the network.

Those contacts that were retained in the final core working network were accorded this status because of their involvement in the main activities under analysis for both case studies. For Marks, the exercise was straightforward in that any contacts documented as having participated within any of the cannabis importation ventures that served as that case study's outcome generator were not removed in the elimination process.

Gravano's activities were not as easily segmented. His street crime activities at the beginning of his career usually came in sprees and his racketeering operations had the same temporal flow, making it difficult to identify separate outcomes. Because Gravano was generally involved in systematic, routine operations in his criminal endeavours, the career outcomes had to be located elsewhere. His organizational affiliation with the Gambino family offered a solution, in that promotions within the family demarcated key transitions throughout his career as well as providing him with opportunities to elaborate his earning activities. The various promotions that Gravano obtained throughout his career and that helped shape the nature of his activities were therefore held as suitable outcomes indicating his achievements at various points in time. I will elaborate on the promotional aspect of Gravano's career in a later section; for now, it is necessary only to note that those of Gravano's contacts who were not removed from his core working network were persons who were in proximity to his earning operations around and at the time of each of his promotions.

Constructing Marks' Core Working Network

An initial extraction of all names from Marks' autobiography yielded a total of 323 different people that he mentioned throughout his account (see Table 3.1; names appear in the order in which they emerge in *Mr. Nice*).

Table 3.1 Initial Name Extraction and Coded Eliminations from Marks (1997)

Mother (3)	**Dutch Nik**	M. Hemingway (1)
Father (3)	**Dutch Pete**	B. Cornfield (1)
Sister (3)	**P. Lane**	J. Lennon (1)
M. Langford	**J. Lane**	M. Jagger (1)
A. Hancock (4)	R. O'Hanlon (4)	Sabrina (2)
P.C. Hamilton (7)	**B. O'Hanlon**	Miranda (2)
H.J. Davies (2)	A. Woodhead (4)	A. Guinness (2)
R. Meiggs (2)	**A. Woodhead**	J.B. Carter (2)
J. Peto (4)	M. Bell (4)	R. Fraser (2)
George (2)	D. Thomas (4)	Harvey (2)
D.L. Keir (2)	A. Marcuson (2)	F. Amadi (2)
J. Minford (2)	M. Lessor (2)	A. Malmik (2)
H. McMillan (5)	R. Neville (2)	P. Ustinov (1)
D. Irving (4)	**J. McCann**	J. Betteridge (2)
W. Bund (2)	C. Richardson (4)	A. Lehmann (2)
George's repl. (2)	B. McCann (6)	N. Douglas (2)
D. Yardley (2)	J. Weaver (6)	P. Slinger (4)
J. Esam (2)	N. Hoogstratten (1)	S. Minford (4)
F. Lincoln (2)	D. Murray (2)	M. O'Connell (4)
A. Montefore (2)	R. Murray (5)	R.D. Laing (2)
S. Balogh (2)	Eamonn (6)	L. Watson (2)
G. Friesm (2)	Gus (6)	**S. Malik**
I. Kadegis (4)	**Raoul**	P. Whitehead (5)
Dia (4)	**E. Combs**	Mohammed (6)
G. Plinston	M. Jardine (4)	Willy (6)
H. Weightman (4)	**'Old Oxford**	**S. Prentiss**
Uncle Mostyn (3)	**Acquaintance'**	**N. Lane**
B. Jefferson (4)	**Eric**	**Sharif**
C. Lee (4)	Donald (2)	P.J. Proby (2)
M. Dummett (2)	R. Carr (4)	T. Baker (2)
J. Sparrow (2)	**J. Gater**	D. Campbell (2)
J. Stein (2)	Arend (4)	E. Clamp (6)
F. Hill Stein (4)	**G. Lickert**	**S. Trafficante**
C. Hill (4)	A. McNulty (4)	S. Giancana (1)
C. Logue (1)	Silvia (4)	D. Goldsmith (4)
B. Patten (1)	**J. Morris**	B. Jagger (1)
J. Martin	B. Simons (5)	J. Magazine (6)
G. Martin (4)	B. Moldese (6)	W. Nath (6)
J. Giedymin (2)	P. Fairweather 2)	B. Kenningale (6)
Lebanese Joe	Patty (4)	N. Baker (7)
R. Lewis (2)	**R. Crimball**	T. Byrne (7)
Rosie	**J. Denbigh**	N. Cole (6)
M. Plinston (4)	**T. Sunde**	A. Grey (6)
K. Becker (6)	C. Gambino (1)	H. Morgan (6)
M. Durrani	**C. Galante (4)**	J. Kern (2)
S. Hiraoui	**D. Brown**	R. Knight (2)
D. Pollard	R. Sherman	B. Windsor (2)
Jarvis	**P. Sparrowhawk**	D. Arif (2)
C. Radcliffe	M. Ratledge (4)	D. Arif (2)
C. Weatherley	A. Tunnicliffe (4)	T. Wiskey (2)
D. Laurie	**L. Ippolito**	**M. Williams**
J. Goldsack	J. Coburn (1)	**S. Hobbs**
T. Radcliffe (4)	B. Coburn (1)	L. Hutchinson (5)
Lang	**A. Schwarz**	J. del Rio (2)

Table 3.1 (*Concluded*)

M. Stephenson (7)	E. Marcos (1)	G. Rodriguez (2)
Leaf (4)	R. Cruz (2)	G. Badalementi (2)
P. Rogers (7)	F. Marcos (1)	W. Lovato (2)
J. Rogers (7)	B. Marcos (1)	T. Lundy (7)
S. Solley (5)	**G. Wills**	Zacarias (2)
J. Miskin (6)	Wyonna (4)	Claude (2)
Masha (3)	**Daniel**	Pierre (2)
Appleton (7)	**R. Allen**	Juan (2)
J. Fort (2)	H.D. Yi (2)	D. Bufalino (2)
Ronnie (2)	X. Hing (2)	M. Lane (3)
P.P. Reid (1)	P. Brooke (2)	P. Khalid (2)
S. Rosenthal (2)	L. Bethall (2)	El Fiscal (7)
Price (7)	Ellie (2)	Gustavo (2)
Spencer (7)	Eddie (4)	Marcus (2)
Liz (4)	R. Robb (6)	G.E. Lynch (5)
M. Pocock (5)	Brian (4)	F. Losada (7)
Kathy (5)	D. Embley (4)	J. Parry (2)
D. Leigh (5)	G. Kenion (4)	J. Paine (7)
H. Rubenstein (5)	Justo (2)	B. Lee (2)
Heinemann (5)	Pritchard (7)	D. Re (5)
M.B. Smith (7)	**R. Reaves**	F. Nugan (2)
Dr. Punt (5)	C. Lovato (7)	M. Hand (2)
J.P. Belmondo (1)	**B. Light**	S. Bronis (5)
R. Polanski (1)	**Frederick**	A. Acceturo (2)
N. Kinnock (1)	R. Llofriu (7)	Mona (5)
Balendo (5)	A. Scalzo (7)	P. Eddy (2)
S. Ng (5)	M. Khadri (2)	S. Walden (2)
J. Warren	I. Donaldson (5)	C. Olgiati (2)
L. Moynihan	Nesty (2)	M. Berg (2)
Sompop (2)	J. Lee (2)	K. Reaves (4)
B. Aitken	Maria (2)	W. Pearson (7)
A. Chung (2)	R. Richards (2)	G. Langella (2)
April (2)	M. Katz (2)	J. Nolan (2)
Selena (2)	L. Pina (2)	J. Carneglia (2)
R. Webborn (5)	P. Gibbons (2)	V. Amuso (2)
Flash	Marie (4)	F. Locascio (2)
Bill	Nigel (3)	A. Indelicato (2)
S. Sherman (6)	J. Morell (5)	A. Aiello (2)
S. Tailor (6)	Rafael (2)	J. Testa (2)
S. Alraji (4)	B. O'Neill (7)	J. Coonan (2)
Aftab (6)	Pres. Zia (1)	L. Fiocconi (2)
H.L. Bowe (7)	T. Cash (7)	V. Bower (2)
Carl	J. Mejuto (7)	Webster (7)
Orca (5)	T. Caballero (2)	T.B. Taylor (2)
D. Jenkins (4)	J. Francis (2)	Jacobi (2)
F. Hillard	B. Daniels (2)	R. Bonner (7)
B. Edwards (2)	B. Alexander (2)	B. Clinton (1)
G. Lane (3)	R. Brown (2)	Bear (2)
A. O'Brien (3)	J. Canavaggio (2)	D. Roche (2)
Spencer (7)	J. Ochoa (2)	W. Griffith (2)
Editha (4)	F. Ochoa (1)	J. Yacoub (2)
J. Newton	M. Ochoa (1)	J. Jones (2)
Helen (2)	C. Lehder (1)	J. Meko (7)
J. Smith	P. Escobar (1)	T. Burke (7)

Once all names were extracted, I began the elimination process. A considerable number of the people referred to in *Mr. Nice* were mentioned only in contextualizing the period within which Marks was describing an event. Several others were simply famous people that he came across while conducting his business activities. None were part of Marks' proximate social entourage and, in many cases, Marks never even met them. This was the first group to be removed from the initial set. The 26 names that fall into this category are coded '1' in Table 3.1.

The second set of contacts that were eliminated from the initial 323 names comprised people that Marks briefly met at various stages throughout his career and who left no impact whatsoever in regard to Marks' cannabis trade activities (coded '2' in Table 3.1). Inmates that Marks encountered during his prison spells and who had no additional link to any of his cannabis trade activities were included in this group. In all, 117 names were eliminated under this criterion.

Contacts that are coded '3' in Table 3.1 are family members who maintained no business links with Marks, 9 of whom were removed in this selection. Also, 43 friends who maintained no business links with Marks were removed from the remaining set of contacts (coded '4'). Friends and family of these friends and family were included within these two categories.

The fifth set of contacts that were eliminated in this selection process comprised people with whom Marks had maintained business links, but with whom he had no relation within the context of his illicit endeavours (coded '5'). Lawyers throughout Marks' career who had no direct involvement in the operations extending from his cannabis trade ventures were also included in this group. Of the remaining names, 22 fitted this criterion.

Several people were mentioned throughout the account that were associated with others implicated in Marks' cannabis trade ventures, albeit in an indirect manner (direct link of Marks' direct link) and only to a minimal extent; this group was coded '6.' A clear example of this set of eliminated contacts is the case of B. Moldese, who once brought Marks $100 000 from E. Combs, one of Marks' main cannabis trade contacts. Although Moldese may have been associated with the cannabis trade activities at that point, he was not a 'core' contact at that or any other time throughout Marks' career. In all, 20 contacts were removed under this criterion.

The final set of 28 excluded names consisted of law enforcement, judicial, or correctional officials that Marks came across (coded '7'). This left 58 contacts (in boldface in Table 3.1) that were directly implicated in the various cannabis trade activities described. These contacts served as the pool of network nodes for the various analyses throughout the Marks case study.

Constructing Gravano's Core Working Network

Overall, 249 names were mentioned at least once in Gravano's biography (Maas 1997). Once again, names do not necessarily qualify as contacts. All individuals who were referred to but whom Gravano never met or who were simply mentioned as contextual references were removed. These included figures who were temporally, geographically, or relationally detached from Gravano but whose reputations and own experiences were referred to in various anecdotes (e.g., Al Capone, Lucky Luciano, Frankie Yale). A total of 41 names fit this criterion (code '1' in Table 3.2).

Gravano records 40 contacts with people who were briefly encountered throughout his career or had no impact on his earning activities and entrepreneurial progression (code '2'). Family members who had no business links with Gravano were coded '3' (10 contacts) and eliminated. Another 10 were removed from the contact list as friends of a non-business nature (code '4').

Non-criminal business links (code '5') also made up a group of 10 contacts. Note, however, that 'legitimate' contacts that were implicated in Gravano's racketeering activities (illegal practices in legitimate business settings) were not removed under this criterion.

An additional 49 contacts were eliminated because their involvement in Gravano's criminal activities was not direct or extensive enough to warrant classification within his core working network (code '6'). Most of the contacts in this relatively large group were others who were documented as members in various Cosa Nostra families. For example, Gravano mentioned his interactions with a wide array of Cosa Nostra members in New York City and elsewhere, but never revealed any real working relationships with them. Such contacts did not occupy a place within his core working network. Although there is no proof that these contacts were indeed participants in Gravano's own criminal activities, the overlapping social web that knits together the various collective units in the Cosa Nostra does permit us to document them as criminal participants in proximity to the central character.

Table 3.2 Initial Name Extraction and Coded Eliminations from Maas (1997)

J. Profaci (1)	R. Spero	Stymie D'Angelo
J. Colombo	G. Langella (6)	**J. Paruta**
F. Yale (1)	S. Albanese (6)	**V. Oil**
A. Capone (1)	A.B. Persico (6)	tipster (6)
C. Gravano (3)	H. McIntosh (6)	**Ma. DeBatt**
G. Gravano (3)	Butchy (2)	**Mi. DeBatt**
Zuzito (2)	De. Scibetta (3)	JoJo (2)
Mandracchia (2)	Di. Scibetta (3)	Biker (2)
L. Gallo (1)	J. Zicarelli (3)	C. Fatico (6)
J. Gallo (1)	**A.B. Cuomo**	E. Gambino (1)
J. Emma	**M. Hardy**	J. McBratney (1)
G. Pappa	J. Brassiere (6)	R. Galione (2)
Joe V.	**S. Aurello**	R. Cohn (2)
T. Snake	J. Valachi (1)	**R. DeMeo**
Lenny the Mole	N. Scarfo (6)	S. Maggadino (1)
Benocchio (7)	Karen (3)	S. Giancana (1)
Lawyer 1 (5)	Gerard (3)	N. Civella (1)
Lorraine (4)	**E. Garafola**	J. Scalish (1)
Nick the Baker (4)	Dominick (2)	L. Trafficante (1)
L. Grimaldi (4)	Danny (5)	J. Ida (1)
Little Louie (4)	M. Perry (5)	F. DiSimone (1)
J. Grimaldi (4)	Dunn Br. 1 (2)	J. Lanza (1)
L. Milito	Dunn Br. 2 (2)	P. Conte (6)
T. Spero	L. Martieri (6)	P. Castellano Jr. (2)
Dutchie (2)	E. Gold (7)	J. Castellano (2)
G. LaTorroca (2)	J. Bonnano (1)	Ph. Castellano (2)
Frannie (3)	**A. Dellacroce**	F. Perdue (1)
D. Scialo (2)	T. Anastasio (1)	J. O'Brien (7)
J. Vitale (2)	A. Scotto (6)	T. Salerno (6)
T. Shorty Spero	R.F. Kennedy (1)	F. Mosca (6)
L. Luciano (1)	T. Gambino (6)	**J. Watts**
V. Genovese (1)	**P. Castellano**	**V. Di Napoli**
F. Costello (1)	A. Gaggi (6)	**R. DiBernardo**
A. Anastasia (1)	D. Gaggi (6)	**J. Madonia**
C. Gambino	**J. Gotti**	**L. DiBono**
C. Persico Jr.	J. Gotti Jr. (6)	**J. Cody**
J. Colombo Jr. (2)	**A. Ruggiero**	**B. Sasso**
A. Colombo (2)	C. Aurello (6)	D. Trump (1)
Frankie	F. the Wop (6)	J. Luciano (5)
R. Ronga	**J.N. Gallo**	J. Simone (2)
J. Colucci	**J. Failla**	A. Bruno (1)
Sam 'Plumber'(2)	**F. DiCicco**	T. Bananas (1)
B. Stagg	**B. DiCicco**	P. Testa (1)
J. Rizzo	**T. Bilotti**	**N. Russo**
M. Gambino	N.Scibetta (3)	**P. Joey**
N. Rockefeller (1)	T. Jets (6)	F. Steele (1)
Camille (4)	G. DiCicco (6)	C. Gigante (6)

Table 3.2 (*Concluded*)

Salty (6)	N. Castellano (4)	B. Boriello (6)
Vinnie Sicilian (6)	D. Shacks (6)	J. D'Angelo Jr. (4)
T. Carbonaro	**J. Armone**	**P. Gotti**
J. Skaggs (5)	J. Corrao (6)	J. Giordano (6)
F. Fiala (2)	E. Garafalo (6)	B. Mangano (6)
J. Ingrassia (6)	L. Giardino (6)	V. Amuso (6)
N. Mormando	F. Piccolo (6)	V. Orena (6)
N. Gravanti (5)	N. Auletta (6)	J. Bilotti (6)
G. Shargel (5)	C. Marcello (1)	Johnny G. (2)
T. Scarpatti (6)	R. Giuliani (7)	A. Squitieri (2)
J.E. Hoover (1)	A. Corallo (6)	N. Pileggi (1)
G.R. Blakey (1)	P. Rastelli (6)	Fat Bobby (2)
W. Webster (7)	J. Messino (6)	J. Amico (6)
J. Kallstrom (7)	A. Casso (6)	J. Miller (1)
B. Mouw (7)	J. La Rossa (7)	J. O'Connor (2)
S. Ruggiero (6)	D. Marino (6)	G. Gabriel (7)
G. Gotti	**J. Alogna**	A. Maloney (7)
J. Carneglia	**V. Artuso**	R. Morgenthau (7)
T. Rampino	S. Ciccone (6)	J. Gleeson (7)
S. Scala	E. McCarthy (1)	Gina (3)
E. Lino	F.H. Bellino (2)	B. Saccente (2)
W.B. Johnson (6)	A. Aronne (2)	R. Snipes (1)
J. Favara (2)	Butterass (2)	Diane (4)
F. Gotti (2)	Oscar (2)	Norman (2)
Dino	Paulie (2)	J. Fox (7)
J. Polito	F. Spero (7)	I.L. Glasser (7)
M. Mastromari	M. Tricorio (7)	A. Krieger (5)
Ja. Colucci	R. Piecyk (2)	S. Bronfman (5)
R. Scopo	F. Colletta (2)	A. D'Arco (6)
M. Carbone	D. Giacalone (7)	A. Quinn (1)
E.J. Halloran (6)	O. North (1)	M. Rourke (1)
S. LeFrak (2)	**F. Locascio**	A. Cardinale (5)
J. Kravec (7)	B. Cutler (7)	L. Ward (7)
J. Cantamessa (7)	**B. Radonjic**	Corrupt juror (2)
J. Bonavolenta (7)	**L. Vallario**	F.L. Bailey (2)
G. Olarte (4)	**L. Saccente**	O.J. Simpson (1)

The final group comprised 22 formal control agents (code '7'). This left us with a core personal working network of 67 contacts (indicated in boldface in Table 3.2).

Career Representations

Once I had identified the core working networks for Marks and Gravano, each contact was identified by the year in which he was documented as having come into contact with the case study's central character. An additional piece of information identified the persons through whom Marks or Gravano met each contact. The combination of when and through whom each contact appeared constituted the basic components used in designing the career working network representations displayed in Figure 4.1 in Chapter 4 and Figure 5.1 in Chapter 5.

The complete scope of both Marks' and Gravano's working networks, and therefore the complete scope of their respective earning activities, may be expected to surpass that documented in Marks' personal account or in the Maas biography of Gravano. It was with this limit in mind that the frame of analysis was narrowed down to the core aspects of their careers. These core aspects are assumed to be indicated by those elements that the central characters perceived as important enough to include in their life history accounts.

Further details on each contact were extracted to establish a temporal evolution of these relational representations. The aim of this time-ordered network representation was to assess the size of each network at various points throughout the career. Information concerning the entrance of each contact into the network was already documented in the creation of the career working networks detailed in the previous section. What was required was additional indication of the year in which each contact exited the criminal entrepreneur's core network.

Contacts exiting Marks' or Gravano's working networks were determined by the last period during which they were mentioned as participants in the general activities under analysis. Some contacts were arrested, imprisoned, and no longer alluded to in later accounts. Others were revealed to have become junkies and unreliable working contacts. Some, particularly in Gravano's case, simply died. Although many of these contacts may be assumed to have been continuous network members, they were no longer introduced as participants in any of the activities or phases in each career. In short, the contact may have remained in social proximity to the criminal entrepreneur, but he no longer warranted the status of a core working network member. With information on both years of entry and exit, I created a cumulative working network distribution of Marks' and Gravano's personal networks from one year to the next.

Aside from contacts, I collected information permitting the ordering of all criminal and legitimate earning activities and events, as well as any confrontations with law enforcement officials, courts, or correctional institutions. For Gravano, whose achievement outcome was indicated by his promotional rank within the Gambino family, additional information was obtained in order to specify the time period in which he climbed from one promotion to the next.

Time-ordered axes were created for each entrepreneur. Through the use of primary and supplementary data sources, I was generally able to situate various events or phases within each thematic sequence by the month (or season) and year. Each axis was constructed of detailed events or phases that made up the particular themes inherent in each criminal entrepreneur's experience.

For Marks, the ensemble of event-based information documented in *Mr. Nice* is illustrated in Figure 4.2 (Chapter 4) and superimposed on his cumulative working network distribution. The three axes in Figure 4.2 identify Marks' cannabis trade scams (Axis 1), arrests and incarcerations (Axis 2), and legitimate or front ventures (Axis 3). Each cannabis trade venture (in Axis 1) is initiated by an entrepreneurial opportunity (E.O.). These entrepreneurial opportunities are represented by co-participants who were directly linked to Marks' capacity to participate in the trade. Fourteen ventures were compiled from the information provided throughout *Mr. Nice*. Venture 1 (V1), for example, had Marks as an initial planner, but was only executable with the addition of Jim McCann (N23 in Figure 4.1). Venture 9, quite differently, had the same E.O. in McCann, but for a scam designed by McCann and offered to Marks. Each venture/scam consists of a series of consignments (ranging from 1 to 10) that were part of the same set-up.

For Gravano, organizational promotions, street crime activities, legitimate/racketeering ventures, and law enforcement experiences represented the axes for his career representation (see Figure 5.2).

Both Marks' and Gravano's respective event or sequence axes were subsequently plotted on the cumulative network curves detailing the evolution of each of the central characters' core working networks. The ensemble of thematic axes and cumulative network curves offers us an indication of the activities of each criminal entrepreneur, the extent of these activities, and the various transitions therein in accordance with an indication of the size of the contact pool along that trajectory. These are essentially criminal career representations that permitted the descriptive aspects of Marks' and Gravano's experiences to be revealed in a concise and detailed way.

Operationalizing Career Outcomes

Burt's structural hole theory requires two initial components: personal networks and outcomes indicating some form of achievement. The immersion of outcomes within the boundaries specified by the personal networks remained specific to each case study. Although the most accurate outcome variable indicating the extent of a criminal entrepreneur's achievement would be a straightforward figure measuring the profits made during a series of events, such information is rarely provided in criminal memoirs on a systematic basis. Alternatives, however, may be identified that provide us with respectable proxies for the financial achievements of a criminal entrepreneur.

For the Marks case study, a consignment-based outcome variable was designed by using the weights of importation consignments. *Mr. Nice* provided details on forty-one cannabis shipments that Marks participated in throughout his career. Complete information on the weight of the shipment was obtained for thirty-five of the forty-one consignments. Estimations for the remaining consignments were established in accordance with the overall design and systematic weight of a larger venture of which the consignment was part. On a number of occasions, for example, there were indications that a 'load' of cannabis referred to a one-ton shipment; consignments within that venture were therefore registered as one-ton loads.

Regarding Marks' personal profits from these importation ventures, valid information was derived for only nineteen consignments. Correlation tests, however, proved strong and positive between the weight of a consignment and the profits obtained by Marks ($r = .97$; $\alpha < .001$). Since individual smuggling profits are generally a percentage cut of successful consignments, weights were therefore deemed as suitable proxies for Marks' financial returns in the trade. These weights were subsequently logged in order to reduce the outlying effects of three considerably large consignments (ten, twenty, and thirty tons).

Once the outcome variable was determined, symmetrical network matrices were designed for each of the forty-one consignments in accordance with the information made available in Marks' account. The fifty-eight contacts that passed the network elimination process outlined above constituted the pool of network nodes on which the consignment-based contact matrices were founded. Connected participants in a given consignment were assigned a direct link (coded '1') in a contact matrix, while unconnected players were indicated by the absence of a direct link (coded '0'). The ensemble of Marks' venture-based contact matrices are in Appendix A.

While achievement in Marks' career could be depicted by focusing on his cannabis trade activities, the greater variation in crimes and the more routine quality that characterized Gravano's racketeering activities made it difficult to replicate the same specific event-oriented network modelling. For the Gravano case study, the operationalization procedures adhered much more closely to those operations used by Burt (1992).

The sixty-seven contacts that passed the elimination process that led to the construction of Gravano's core working network constituted the population for his working pool throughout his career. Symmetrical and valued network matrices were designed for periods at the time of each of his six promotions. These six matrices (see Appendix B) were created to account for the relational circumstances underlying these major transitions throughout the twenty-five years of Gravano's career. Each network matrix was limited to a maximum of twenty contacts that were implicated or influential in Gravano's career at the time of each promotion.

Matrix-generating questions remained consistent with Burt's original format. In building Gravano's twenty-contact personal network from one promotion to the next, I also estimated strength of ties. Consistent with Burt's own estimations,[6] 'especially close' (value = 100) indicated Gravano's closest contacts; 'close' (value = 69) indicated those contacts with whom Gravano maintained a positive personal relation but who were not amongst his closest personal contacts; 'less than close' (value = 37) indicated that Gravano did not mind working with this person but had no desire to develop a friendship (strictly business relationship); and 'distant' (value = 1) indicated that Gravano did not seem to enjoy spending time with this person unless it was necessary. The duration of the relationship had already been established while designing the cumulative working network curve. Frequency of contact was also measured by accounting for whether Gravano talked with contacts on a daily, weekly, monthly, or less frequent basis. Evidently, estimations were required for most cases, but a knowledge of the events, relational

---

6 Further elaboration concerning these tie-strength values may be found in Burt (1992: pp. 287–8 n.2). Burt showed that these values provided an empirically adequate log-linear fit that was also consistent with balance theory principles ('friends of my friends are my friends and enemies of my friends are my enemies').

environment, and working activities at any given period allowed a fair assessment of his frequency of contact with each network member.

Coding relationships between Gravano's contacts also remained consistent with Burt's criteria in that ties were classified either as 'especially close' or 'distant' (in the sense that they rarely worked together, were total strangers, or did not enjoy one another's company). Any relationship deemed to fall between these two extreme classifications was grouped within a mid-range relational strength category. The focus of analysis was therefore based on those 'especially close' (value = 100), 'mid-range' (value = 34), and 'distant' (value = 0) relationships. 'Extreme' relationships were more easily and accurately accounted for than the less distinguishable 'mid-range' ties.

Once all of Marks' cannabis venture networks and Gravano's promotional contact matrices were constructed, the various structural hole properties were calculated[7] and incorporated in the analysis. Subsequent chapters present the analyses that unfolded while applying this method. Once again, the Marks case study served in developing the basic applications. After Burt's structural hole measures and overall framework were found to provide a theoretical fit that accounted for variations in achievement, the method and argument were reapplied to Gravano's experience.

The following chapters present these case studies. Chapters 4 and 5 share a common demonstration. The first and substantial part of the chapter is devoted to a detailed description of the career and the place of contacts therein. The second and less lengthy part of the chapter applies structural hole theory in demonstrating how criminal achievement is intrinsically related to personal network dynamics. Chapter 6 builds off the Gravano case study in demonstrating how violence and network capacities interplay throughout some criminal careers.

---

7 I used UCINET 5.0 (Borgatti, Everett, and Freeman 1999) in constructing the network matrices and in calculating the structural hole measures.

4 Structuring Mr. Nice

In July 1988, Dennis Howard Marks (a.k.a. Donald Nice, Brendan McCarthy, Stephen McCarthy, Peter Hughes, Anthony Tunnicliffe) was arrested by members of the Spanish National Police at his residence in Palma de Majorca, Spain. This arrest was the beginning of a judicial process that would have him extradited to the United States for prosecution under charges including conspiracy, money laundering, and participation in Racketeering-Influenced Corrupt Organizations (RICO). Following a two-year battle against his extradition and the charges laid against him in the United States, Marks pleaded guilty to racketeering and conspiracy to racketeer. He was subsequently sentenced to two consecutive terms of ten and fifteen years. After serving seven years at Terre Haute Penitentiary, he was released in April 1995 and immediately returned to England.

The investigation targeting Marks and the charges brought against him were rooted in a lengthy task force operation, known as 'Operation Eclectic,' headed by members of the Drug Enforcement Agency (DEA) in alliance with domestic police forces from various countries (the United Kingdom, Canada, the United States, the Netherlands, Pakistan, Philippines, Hong Kong, Thailand, Portugal, and Australia). The law-enforcement tandem built a case against Marks alleging that he was responsible for a series of cannabis-smuggling schemes across international borders dating as far back as 1970. Marks was argued to be the principal member of an international cannabis-smuggling ring, referred to as the 'Marks Cartel,' that DEA officials claimed was responsible for 15 per cent of the cannabis entering the United States throughout the seventies and eighties.

Marks was indeed a cannabis trade participant for two decades. His capacity to persist on a consistent basis in the trade, however, was not achieved at the helm of any international smuggling cartel.[1] Marks wasn't even a member of a cartel; nor was he a member of any fixed criminal organization. He was not part of a monopolist nor an oligopolist attempt to control the cannabis trade at any level or in any region of the world. He was a liberal-minded, free-willed, and independent criminal entrepreneur, but an analysis of the inner workings of his cannabis-smuggling activities brings us to see that there was a structure to this apparent disorganization. This structure came in the form of the personal working network that, in its own waxing and waning, embedded his career in the international cannabis trade.

Howard Marks' career is that of a cannabis trade participant who entered the business through an Oxford-based basin of strong ties during the late sixties, effectively and efficiently expanded an already prosperous working set of contacts throughout the early seventies, worked his way to a privileged brokerage position between importer and exporter links in the distribution chain during the latter half of the seventies, attempted to retire to legitimate life in 1982, returned to the trade in 1983, and finally fell to a multinational tandem of law enforcement agencies after his return to cannabis smuggling. This chapter traces the network processes that led to his acquiring, maintaining, and losing a pivotal brokerage position in criminal enterprise.

Academic Background

Marks' story begins in his native Wales, but his initial encounters with the cannabis trade are revealed in his years as an undergraduate and graduate student at Oxford's Balliol College. This Oxford background figured decisively throughout his account because it was there that one may say it all started. He entered Oxford in 1963 and, as he himself stated, 'My success went completely to my head, and I have been living off it to some extent ever since' (Marks 1997: p. 32). This and later successes, as will be demonstrated, had both positive and negative effects throughout the evolution of his career. At Oxford, Marks became a popular figure on campus, grew acquainted with the mid-sixties drug culture, and took his first steps into the cannabis trade.

---

1   A cartel is defined as 'a conspiracy in restraint of trade, an illegal clique of businesses determined to restrict quantity, divide up the market and push up prices' (Naylor 1995: p. 40).

The core of Marks' wholesaling and early importation working group was made up of what he referred to as an 'odd collection of Welsh drop-outs and Oxford academics' (p. 105). Many members of this nucleus of Marks' early working network remained participants in various ventures well into his career. Others withdrew from the trade after they were arrested, incarcerated, or became junkies. The old boys' network that Marks was such a key part of at Oxford opened up several opportunities throughout his career as a cannabis trade entrepreneur.

Marks was able to make contact with key exporters in a matter of two short years in the trade, shifting from retail dealer to wholesaler within the same period. It was through the friends and acquaintances he made at Oxford that he sowed the seeds of what would become his working network for two decades to follow.

Network Expansion as an Importation Coordinator

Adler and Adler (1983) found that middle-level-entry traffickers, as opposed to less ambitious low-level-entry dealers, were more likely to advance and expand in the trade through their access to established dealing friends who allowed the newcomer access to the scene and its fast-paced lifestyle: 'Individuals who found this lifestyle attractive became increasingly drawn to the subculture, building networks of social associations within it' (p. 98).

Marks' experience is indicative of this pattern. He entered the cannabis trade in an apprentice-like relationship with his principal hashish dealer, Graham Plinston, whom he met at Oxford during the mid-sixties and remained in contact with while gradually shifting from a relatively heavy cannabis consumer (twenty joints per day) to a progressively more popular provincial retail dealer and then to a London wholesale coordinator[2] and transnational courier.

Concentrated Contact Allotment

Figure 4.1 shows Marks' personal network members throughout his twenty-year career; Plinston (N3) was the largest contact provider. Only Ernie Combs (N26), Plinston's and Marks' main American importer, approached Plinston's network provision to Marks. Almost half of the

---

2 The concepts of 'coordinator' and, later, 'liaison' and 'representative' are based on Gould and Fernandez's (1989) brokerage classification.

Figure 4.1 Marks' Career Working Network

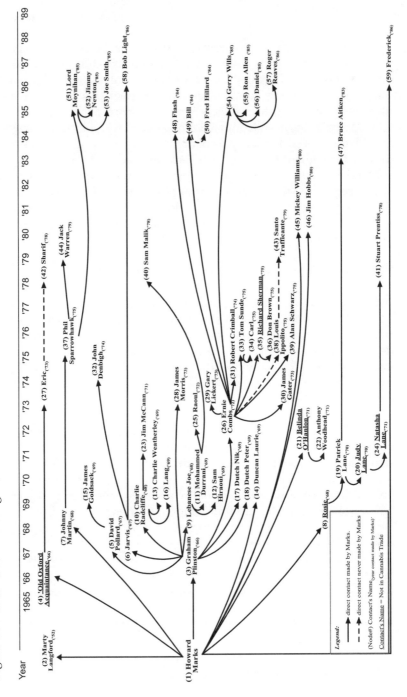

contacts in Figure 4.1 came either from Marks' direct encounters (ten contacts; 17.2 per cent), indirectly through Plinston (eight contacts; 13.8 per cent), or through Combs (ten contacts; 17.2 per cent). Such concentrated contact allotment (high accumulation of eventual contacts extending from a relatively small number of network providers) should be somewhat expected in that the consequences of product illegality limit not only the scope and size of criminal organizations and consistent working groups (Reuter 1983), but also the boundaries within which criminal entrepreneurs have to work – that being the size and amplifying qualities of their networks of potential co-participants, accomplices, and information sources.

Plinston figured even more prominently in Marks' career when we take into account that Marks met Combs through him. From the eight working ties in Figure 4.1 that Plinston put into contact with Marks grew an additional thirty-six network members, resulting in 4.5 (36/8) subsequent ties per tie already made. Combs' contribution proved much lower at 1.7 (17/10). In many ways, Plinston *made* Marks in the cannabis trade, but not in the ritualized, formalized, and required exchange that is often found in more traditional organized crime contexts. In Marks' business, being 'made' meant gaining direct access to the resources of the maker. One may have been expected to return a favour, but such reciprocity was neither absolute nor enforced.

The business relationship between Plinston and Marks eventually grew from a strict apprenticeship to a partnership. Both had become independent British cannabis importers in 1970 when they made contact, through Radcliffe (N10), with James McCann (N23), an IRA member and gun-smuggling, pot-smoking 'living legend' who was ready and able to import hashish sent by Plinston's export contacts. Ventures 1 to 3 (see Axis 1 in Figure 4.2) represent these initial importation ventures with McCann and the onset of the building phase of Marks' career. It was between 1971 and the turn of 1974–5 that Marks made his own place and reputation amongst an increasingly propagating web of business ties in the trade.

Vouched Network Expansion

Tremblay (1993) has argued that 'the search for suitable co-offenders involves the attempt to combine two goals: the search for the strongest ties possible with co-offenders so as to minimize the chances of betrayal and failure; and the search for weak but useful ties so as to increase the scope and value of crime opportunities' (pp. 26–7). Marks, during this building phase, succeeded in using a few strong ties to reach towards weaker, yet vouched for, ties.

During the five-year period encompassing the building phase of his career (1971–5), Marks' working network increased from fourteen to a twenty-contact peak in 1975 (see cumulative working network backdrop to Figure 4.2). Twenty-nine new contacts were added to the network during this period, while twelve exited. The co-participants entering this already prosperous network are indicated in Figure 4.1. Expansion during the first three years of this period was largely due directly or indirectly to Plinston (N3), who gave Marks his links to various exporters in Pakistan (N11 and N25) and Lebanon (N12), as well as to a motley set of other co-participants.

While an increase of six contacts between 1971 and 1975 may seem meagre as an indicator of network building, the fact that Marks was operating within early links in the drug distribution chain must be emphasized. The ensemble of suppliers and clients increases as the distribution chain nears the street level or final sale to the actual consumer. Within and around the importation link in the distribution chain, an addition of six new contacts and indirect access to contacts in their respective personal networks substantially increase one's pool of potential opportunities. Also, network expansion and exposure is a delicate matter amongst criminal trade participants. Six new contacts means six additional persons who are aware of your illegal activities and who may diffuse such knowledge across their respective personal networks. This building phase required that Marks open his network to further contacts and opportunities, affording him increased and quicker access to information useful in seizing more lucrative opportunities. Unlike in legitimate contexts, however, the illegal setting renders the task of searching for new contacts a more constrained and selective process.

Furthermore, the twenty-contact peak from 1975 to 1977 and the fifteen-contact average throughout his career coincides with findings and estimations made by Adler (1993), who found that smuggling crews were generally composed of three to eight members (p. 81). Marks was not a member of any specific crew of smugglers. He had a consistent pool of contacts in place to turn to when necessary, but whom he dealt with varied from venture to venture. If one considers that Marks was involved in roughly two ventures per year (assuming that the entire venture was executed with the same co-participants) and that the numbers involved in each venture corresponded to Adler's

Figure 4.2 Marks' Career Representation

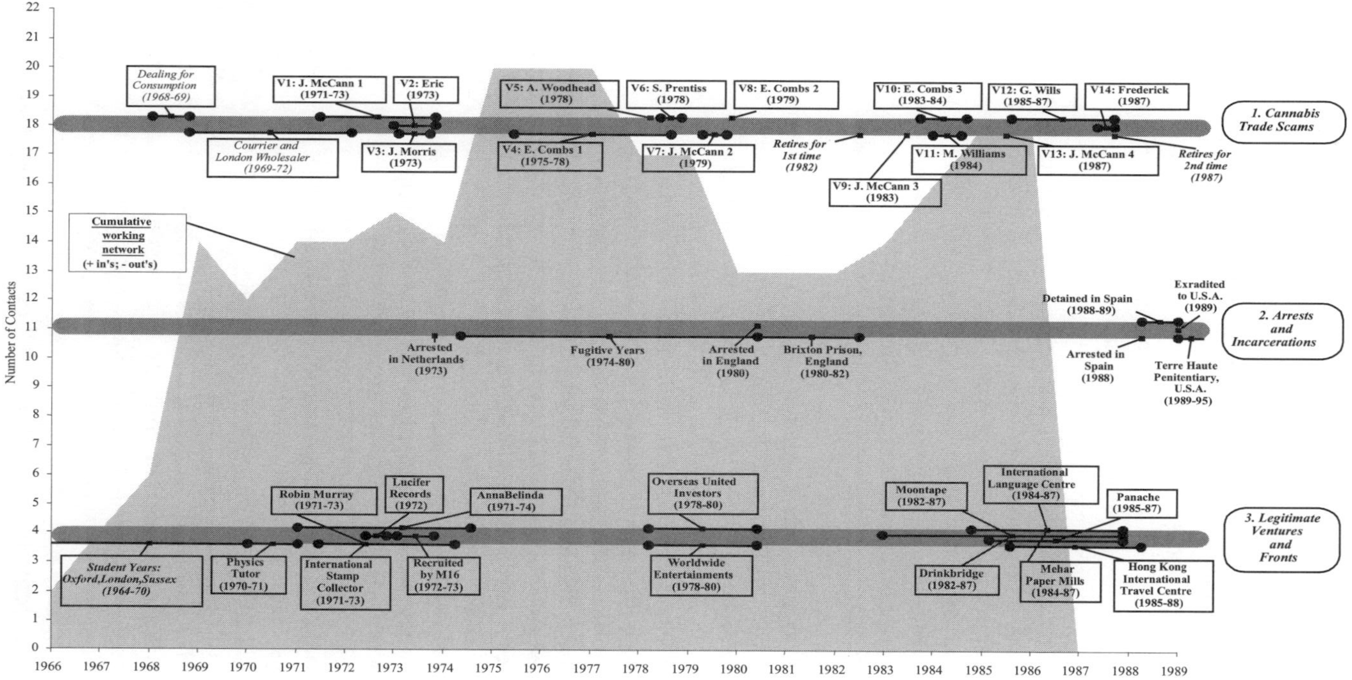

own findings, then the autobiographical information may be taken as offering reasonable estimates for a participant operating in or around the importation segment of cannabis distribution.

Greater access to information and therefore opportunities, as Granovetter (1974) pointed out in his study on legitimate job searchers, is a result of the number of weak ties in one's personal network. For criminal entrepreneurs, dealing with weak ties is necessary if one seeks to increase opportunities and achieve upward mobility, for similar reasons as in legitimate arenas of action. However, in another contrast to legitimate actors or players, such network expansion increases the risk of exposure and of defection on the part of weakly linked co-participants. Building one's reputation and increasing the scope of one's opportunities and activities in criminal networks calls for ambitious participants to take such risks. Marks succeeded in surviving this precarious stage of an increasingly international cannabis trade career. He was also able to come out of it all with strong links with both exporters and importers. Marks, however, had the 'illegitimate means' (Cloward and Ohlin 1960) to seize new opportunities to begin with in that all new working contacts were encountered through an already established contact. All were new and weak ties, but all were also contacts that were vouched for by established members of his working network, with most, once again, having their relational roots with Graham Plinston (N3). Marks consistently used those people that were already relationally in place to advance his own career. Some mutual contacts were weaker ties than others (e.g., meeting N27 through N4 in contrast to meeting N32 through N6 or N26 through N3), but the vouch was nevertheless present and necessary.

It may well be that personal networks amply filled with new and vouched-for opportunities are far from reachable for most participants in illicit trades. That Marks had access to such a network and was able to maintain and further improve the make-up of this network for cannabis trade purposes was a sign of his force in the cannabis trade. Which position one finds oneself in and what one's role becomes in any given trade involving the distribution of illegal goods and services has much to do with whom one knows and how one is able to depend on and use a network of contacts to better one's place within the trade. Money and wealth are clearly facilitators for such upward mobility, but without the social capital in place to convince others to trust and accept participants with high financial capital as investors, partners, or associates, it remains questionable whether any cooperation will emerge.

Marks had, first and foremost, the social capital to participate on a full-time basis in the trade; financial capital soon followed.

Bypassing the Maker

Early ventures generally had Plinston dealing with Combs (e.g., V3 in Figure 4.2). While still partnering with Plinston (N3), Marks began communicating directly with Combs (N26), which eventually led to the two establishing a direct business relationship for later consignments in the same scam. The partnership with Plinston, at that point, went through some important changes. Plinston had continued side-dealing with the erratic Jim McCann (N23), while Marks was more hesitant about pursuing unnecessary risks with this Irish importer. Curiously, it was McCann, during the initial venture (V1 in Figure 4.2), who first tried to convince Marks to operate without Plinston. At that time, Marks was quite aware of the value of Plinston's resources, as his response to McCann tells us: 'Jim, we need Graham. I don't know anyone else who can send stuff from Pakistan and Afghanistan' (Marks 1997: p. 88). Marks eventually attained such contacts through Plinston. Three years later, he was in a position to operate without him.

Marks focused his business on Combs' American importation schemes, and this eventually developed into a complete bypassing of Plinston's involvement: 'Ernie [Combs] gave me $100,000 for my assistance. Graham [Plinston] said that I could keep it all. He wouldn't interfere with any deal I made with Ernie as long as I did not interfere with deals he intended doing with McCann. We would remain partners on all other deals and could invest in each other's individual deals without participation' (p. 119).

This was the beginning of the end of the partnership with Plinston, who had become a redundant contact for Marks the moment that a direct working link was established with Combs. Through one strong tie (N3), Marks accessed a series of key trade participants that further developed his status, abilities, and reputation amongst other players. Plinston's influence may not have been the sole explanation for Marks' ascendancy in the trade, but it is difficult to see how this progression could have occurred without his presence and network allotment.

Plinston had fallen completely out of Marks' working network by 1974, but not before putting Marks in contact with key and reliable exporters from producing/exporting nations and leaving him a strong contact with an established importer in the United States: Plinston's

Pakistani exporter Durrani (N11) and his associate Raoul (N25), his Lebanese exporters Sam Hiraoui (N12) and Lebanese Joe (N9), and his American importer Ernie Combs (N26). This list also includes a wide array of other useful contacts that were able to move and distribute cannabis across international borders and within the boundaries of the United Kingdom.

While Adler and Adler (1983) have explained that the specific social milieu within which their own cannabis and cocaine traffickers resided and operated 'facilitated forming connections and doing business at the upper levels of the drug world' (p. 198), this analysis of Marks' building experience demonstrates how such ascendancy in an illegal trade may be a function less of cultural and more of relationally embedded individual purposive actions. The individual, in this sense, is not offered a subculturally defined set of opportunities to seize as much as he makes the most of those resources that extend from his own personal network.

Figure 4.2 shows that Marks was arrested in the Netherlands in 1973. This arrest was linked to the Rock-Group scam (V3), which involved the smuggling of cannabis into the United States through the concert speakers of early seventies rock groups. Marks was transferred to England for prosecution, granted bail after three weeks in Brixton Prison, and headed for a minimum three-year sentence. He eventually skipped bail. This context is described as follows: 'I had just skipped bail. The trial had started without me the previous day, May 1, 1974. My co-defendants pleaded guilty and got sentences ranging from six months to four years. Ernie [Combs] had promised to pay off any sureties demanded by the judge as the result of my skipping bail. He felt indebted to me because at the time of my arrest in Amsterdam I was the only person in the world who knew his whereabouts, and I had not disclosed them to the authorities ' (Marks 1997: p. 130). For the next six-and-a-half years, Marks would flourish in the cannabis trade while remaining a fugitive from the law.

Attaining Positional Privilege: Liaison and Representative Brokering

The network of exporters, importers, wholesale distributors, and other trusting co-participants that Marks successfully put together through his apprenticeship and partnering with Plinston had become an efficient relational working base for a cannabis trade smuggler. By the turn of 1974–5, Marks had reached his peak in terms of network expansion (see cumulative working network distribution in Figure 4.2). While Burt (1992) and Granovetter (1973, 1974) argue that larger networks are more effective in attempting to increase potential opportunities extending from weak ties or non-redundant contacts (larger networks increase the potential for both types of contacts), the criminal entrepreneur is often faced with upper boundaries in regard to expansion. This coincides with the views of Erickson (1981) and Baker and Faulkner (1993), who argue that groups, organizations, and individuals operating under risky and clandestine circumstances are distinct in that the need to maximize security often trumps a desire for efficiency. This peak or limit in network expansion is not necessarily a sign of failure. It may, however, spell failure for those who push the limits further, in that the increased exposure to a wider set of weak, albeit vouched for, ties generates an increased likelihood of exposure to external regulatory agents and defection among co-participants.

For Marks, such weak ties proved useful and reliable until this phase, but he did adapt to those privileged circumstances that were before him at the onset of his fugitive years. One privilege extended from a change in position that had him receiving offers to participate rather than seeking opportunities to initiate, complement, or complete his own coordinating ventures. What other trade members sought from Marks was his ability to act as a liaison between exporting and importing links or as an importation representative among exporters. This *between-link* brokerage position placed Marks in a most advantageous position in that he was able to increase his own security while simultaneously assuring and even increasing the efficiency of his working network.

Between-Link Advantages

According to Adler (1993) and others (Block and Chambliss 1981; Haller 1990; Desroches 2005), few participants in drug dealing, trafficking, and smuggling have the capacity to coordinate and meet all resource requirements (i.e., financial, connections, skills, experience) necessary to conduct a successful drug-smuggling venture. However, amongst co-participants, there are positions that give some a competitive and security edge over others.

According to Baker and Faulkner (1993) in their price-fixing study, 'As an agent of a company, an individual conspirator wants to be a *central player* in the illegal network ... Personally, however, an actor wants to be a *peripheral player* (if a player at all) to avoid detection,

prosecution, and sanctioning' (p. 845). It may be assumed that delega-
tion is a common strategy for central players to protect themselves, and
the most privileged (and likely the most cautious) are those who are
able to establish cushions of social contacts between themselves and the
activity under surveillance. Brokers are precisely such peripheral players. They remain relatively distant from the distribution of illegal goods
(hence decreasing the risks of detection) while consistently receiving a
portion of the profits extending from the circulation process. Being at
the centre of the action, in this sense, does not necessarily mean that one
has a privileged role in the distribution process and mobilization procedures across a chain. Social distance from the passage of the illegal
goods in question is an asset in criminal enterprise – it offers a player
ampler insulation and a capacity to invest time and energy in simultaneous ventures.

Such incentives favouring security over efficiency also influence how
the circulation process from one end of a distribution chain to the other
is structured. The business of mobilizers found *within* each link in a
given chain ceases the moment that the illegal commodity moves into
the boundaries of the succeeding link (e.g., from exporter link to importer link). Marks' main Pakistani exporter during the latter part of his
career (Malik: N40) implied this on a series of occasions:

> Where product ends up and with who[m] it ends up is not my concern. I
> meet only you, D.H. Marks. How I give product, you say. How you give
> money, I say. (p. 219)

And:

> My commitment is to you, not to any American. You are most welcome to
> accompany me to NWFP to my tribe's factory near Peshawar in Khyber
> Pass. You can choose quality. You can make inspection. But no American
> can go there ... If you are satisfied, I will bring hashish to Karachi and out
> in warehouse. Then, if you want, you can show to Americans. That is your
> affair. (p. 291)

The drug distribution process is a take-and-give procedure, more
reminiscent of a children's game of hot potato than a formal organizational structuring or centralized control of passage. The privileged positions along the chain go to those players who take part in the action but
also remain distant from the proof that is sought after in law enforce-

ment targeting. Such positioning is illustrated in the liaison or representative brokering that was Marks' place in the trade during his post-Plinston years.

While between-link brokers may be found along various segments of the distribution chain, they are most needed between geographically distant and relationally time-consuming exporting and importing links. Marks' personal network, by 1975, was exquisitely designed for him to seize such a position. Successful illegal trade brokers are those players who are not exclusively dependent on any one participant. Their non-redundant positioning and needed resources dictate that they are more likely sought after by others than vice versa.

Adler (1993), in her assessment of intermediaries or 'middlers,' found evidence of two types of brokering: that initiated by suppliers and that initiated by interested buyers (p. 52). Marks' brokerage experiences were initiated exclusively by buyers (by importers). Although he was not an exclusive insider among either importers or exporters, between-link brokerage opportunities consistently came from importers looking to connect with exporters, whereupon Marks would either represent importers' interests within the exporter link or serve as a connecting vector in liaison fashion. Although Adler found middling to be a 'last resort' form of dealing or a position held by peripheral and struggling dealers who proved 'unable to successfully establish and maintain regular buying and selling connections' (p. 54), a reinterpretation of this brokerage position yields additional insight: because 'the possibilities of making a profit by dealing drugs within any given friendship circle are limited ... it is persons able to bridge otherwise separated groups who are in a particularly profitable position (Ekland-Olson, Lieb, and Zurcher 1984: p. 171). As one of Adler's own interviewees pointed out, brokering is not necessarily a low-status position: 'It's not really dealing – it's just putting together two connections, but the trick is to keep them apart so they don't know who each other are and they need you to complete the link' (1993: p. 54). The trick, in Burt's (1992) terms, is to keep non-redundant contacts non-redundant.

Liaison brokers have a slight advantage over representative brokers in view of their distance from the targeted action. Marks, for example, took on the representative role on several occasions (see quotations from Marks' Pakistani exporter Malik, above). In contrast to those consignments for which he served as a liaison between non-redundant importers-exporters and for which no other investment was required but to connect two within-links, as an importer representative among exporters he was positioned closer to the illegal commodity, albeit in the generally impunitive confines typical of production and exportation regions. Marks' presence in Malik's Afghanistan–Pakistan border operational compound, for example, did place him right in the middle of the action and called for considerable investment of his own time and energy (i.e., testing the drug, assuring logistics of a shipment, and managing costs of importers). However, the risks associated with the representative brokerage position remained much less extensive than those associated with his earlier ventures as a coordinator of importation scams in demand-side regions, such as the United Kingdom or United States. It nevertheless remains true that, of the three possible brokerage positions, the liaison brokerage position is clearly the least time consuming and financially demanding. It is also the most insulated.

Compensating the Sucker's Pay-Off

While all players in a chain make some form of investment, the between-link broker is placed in a privileged position in that although he may invest considerable time and energy, he does not generally make a financial investment in the mobilization process. By investing his social capital (or connecting non-redundant contacts), however, he takes the risks that come with vouching for and securing the financial resources of two otherwise unconnected parties. If one party does not fulfil his part of the brokered contract, it is the broker who becomes responsible for compensating the other party. Although the broker is in a highly profitable position (in terms of financial returns per initial investment) when all turns out well, he risks substantial financial losses if one of his contacts decides to renege on his side of the deal. In a non-contractual setting, such as the cannabis trade, there are consequences of product illegality that are unique to the broker.

Marks explains this arrangement quite clearly:

> There is a general rule in most hashish-smuggling ventures: if the scam gets busted by the authorities, the scam shareholders lose their investment, pay any costs, and no one else is held responsible for the loss. There is another general rule: if there is any kind of rip-off, the shareholders do not lose their investment, get paid their profit, and the person who ripped off is held responsible. The logic is sound: bonding together against the enemy during troubled times but paying the penalty for trusting the wrong person during untroubled times. (Marks 1997: p. 160)

The second of these rules may be modified and labelled the 'broker rule' because if the person behind the rip-off is not found, he who vouched for that person is held responsible. This was Marks' experience when he coordinated a venture between his Pakistani hashish-exporting contacts and Anthony Woodhead (N22), a consistent co-participant in several of Marks' ventures during the building phase of his career. Woodhead, in V5, defected from the venture and was never found. As Marks writes: 'According to the rules, I owed $750,000 to Raoul [N25] and Durrani [N11]' (p. 161). Had the rip-off not occurred, Marks stood to make 25 per cent of $1 000 000 (p. 160) for brokering the deal. His initial financial investment was nil.

Between-link brokers gain a percentage of the profits[3] that would otherwise be split amongst succeeding within-link participants. If one party defects, the broker is fully responsible and losses become considerable. In the rip-off detailed above, this amounted to three times more than the expected reward. The broker is in the business of controlling and assuring type-1 results of the Prisoner's Dilemma (no defectors, or mutual cooperation) in which (directly or indirectly) transacting criminal entrepreneurs consistently find themselves. He pays when the result is a sucker's pay-off (one player defects from the deal). He invests his time and energy making and breaking relations and tending to those who have consistently proven trustworthy and reliable. Although players in subsequent links lose a percentage of their profits by employing someone to broker a deal, their incentive is evident: the broker serves as a buffer between buyers and sellers in the illegal trade while, at the same time, providing a guarantee that their financial investment will pay off whether the consignment runs according to plan or not. In a business lacking the formal and conventional fallbacks for regulating contracts, the use of a broker for within-link participants serves to overcome a large part of the risks.

Network Closure

Marks' positional privilege was the result of a cumulative process of seizing and accessing one entrepreneurial opportunity after another until he himself became the entrepreneurial opportunity to be seized by others. The favourable reputation he established with those players

---

3 Marks' details allow general estimates of approximately 15 per cent of after-sales profits going to liaison brokers and about 20 per cent to representatives.

with whom he was in business, particularly Ernie Combs (N27), aided him in establishing himself as a between-link broker. The mix of becoming an entrepreneurial opportunity for others and his between-link positioning is partly indicated in Figure 4.2 by the stability of his cumulative working network between 1975 and 1977 and the subsequent drop in this distribution throughout the years leading to his arrest in 1980. During this period, Marks' network waned. The twenty-contact peak in Figure 4.2 persisted for three years, dropping to seventeen in 1978 (three new contacts in, six former contacts out) and 1979 (two in, two out) and thirteen in 1980 (two in, six out). This network closure coincides with Marks' fugitive years and the introduction to his network of additional exporters, importers, and investors, as well as other key participants for his various scams.

The ability to select incoming opportunities from such a privileged position means that one may choose to participate only on relatively safe and profitable terms. The drop in cumulative contacts and the consistency in cannabis trade ventures in Figure 4.2 that represented Marks' career from the mid-1970s to 1980 illustrate how he was able to continue participating while at the same time decreasing the overall number of people with whom he had to deal. This tells us that Marks was involved less extensively with new contacts; of those rare new contacts that did enter his network during those years, most were vouched for by Combs. As a between-link broker, Marks was also in direct contact with fewer co-participants per venture. Here, we are able to see the network closure pattern that is a strategic reaction to the formal control and sanctioning process confronting offenders (Ekland-Olson, Lieb, and Zurcher 1984). Although Marks did decrease the number of contacts in his overall working network, his entrepreneurial opportunities did not follow suit – in fact, they increased. Privileged positioning means that one may stay away from the action, work and be in contact with as few other participants as possible, select the choice opportunities that are offered, reap the profits that come with brokering, and dabble simultaneously in a number of similarly designed ventures. This was the networking that structured Marks' trade activities during the height of his career.

The Makings of a Good Scam

The combination of durability, stability, and consistent profit defines the makings of a successful scam. This mix provides the incentives for all players involved in the venture to keep a good thing going; 'If,' as Marks tells us, 'a scam works, it is rational to repeat it' (Marks 1997: p. 266). Marks extends this rationale in a summary of his most successful venture (V4 in Figure 4.2), which was finally busted by the DEA in 1979:

> Between 1975 and 1978, twenty-four loads totaling 55,000 pounds of marijuana and hashish had been successfully imported through John F. Kennedy Airport, New York. They had involved the Mafia, the Yakuza, the Brotherhood of Eternal Love, the Thai army, the Palestine Liberation Organisation, the Pakistani Armed Forces, Nepalese monks, and other individuals from all walks of life. The total profit made by all concerned was $48,000,000. They'd had a good run. (p. 166)

Further details on ten of the twenty-four consignments that made up this particular venture are also provided. These consignments demonstrate how similar are the criteria for success (the 'good thing') in criminal and legitimate forms of enterprise.

Figure 4.3 illustrates the logged weights for all forty-one consignments documented in *Mr. Nice*. The onset of Marks' most successful phase (the attainment phase) begins with consignment 16, the beginning of V4 (see Figure 4.2) in 1975. This phase ends with consignment 30, a busted 1979 scam (V8) that resulted in Marks' subsequent arrest. This phase illustrates a relatively stable operating period in Marks' career. During these years, he was consistently involved in consignments made up of about one thousand kilograms (or three logged kilograms). The first four ventures (V4 to V7 in Figure 4.2) were designed to operate in one-ton standard, and the most successful of these ventures (V4) ran steadily for almost four years with few interruptions. Such stability is less apparent during the building phase and even less so during the final years of Marks' career. The failure of consignment 30 is in itself an indication of the problems that may arise from a more erratic operating system.

Between consignments 16 and 29, Marks prospered in the trade. While his networking and between-link positioning played a considerable role in the endurance of this peak period, Marks had consistently involved himself in scams that more or less fit the same operating model in regard to his own positioning and shipment weights. He was a between-link broker who was most effective in moving one-ton consignments of cannabis.

A good scam is one that can be repeated. The more it can be repeated,

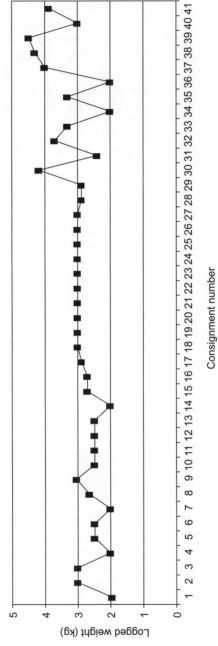

Figure 4.3 Logged Weights of Consignments across Marks' Career

the better the scam. During his attainment phase, Marks experienced operational stability as a criminal entrepreneur. The scam that ended this peak period (consignment 30) had him smuggling fifteen tons of marijuana from Colombia to the United Kingdom. Sizable ventures, if successful, do guarantee the criminal entrepreneur large profits; however, Marks' story tells us that, more than anything else, such over-ambitious venturing led to his downfall. His most successful period repeatedly employed a proven working system, a manageable weight for each shipment, privileged positioning, and regularity, albeit not maximization, in profits.

In 1980, Marks' six-and-a-half-year flight from justice came to an end with an arrest in England following the bust of consignment 30. He spent just over two 'easy' years in Brixton Prison – 'The two years had gone by quickly enough, and I'd beaten the real charge' (p. 194). Upon release, he found himself in a financially sound situation in that most wholesale profits from the unseized portion of the busted consignment had been collected. He took his first retirement, succeeding in remaining fully legitimate for roughly one year before re-entering the trade in 1983.

Going Down: Network Dynamics Structuring an Independent Criminal Entrepreneur's Career

The present section wraps up Marks' career by extending the focus to the final phase of his international cannabis trade endeavours and analysing, with the use of Burt's structural hole measures, the relation between event- and career-based outcomes and personal network strategies. This final phase begins with Marks' decision to re-enter the trade in 1983 and ends with his fall, in 1987, to the international law enforcement tandem that had been targeting his actions and those of his regular co-participants.

Becoming Redundant: Being Bypassed

Although he continued to be solicited by various interested parties to broker or mobilize a deal through his own working network, Marks seemed to have lost the competitive edge he had built and maintained for over ten years. On two occasions, for example, he did exactly what brokers are not supposed to do if they want to remain indispensable. For ventures 11 and 13 (Figure 4.2), he permitted participants between whom he was brokering to contact each other and operate together (N45 and N37 for V11 and N57 and N23 for V13). This naturally led to Marks' exclusion from each scam. His position became obsolete because he gave each player direct access to his social resources. Marks later became aware of what had taken place, as his reaction regarding the first event makes clear: 'So Mickey Williams [N45] had somehow got hold of Phil [N37], and the Dutch air-freight scam had, presumably, been resurrected, this time without me. I couldn't really complain. I didn't really own Phil, and it wasn't I who introduced him to Mickey. But I was glad to know what was going on' (p. 296).

His encounter with Reaves (N57) in 1986 was from the onset marked by a similar faulty brokerage strategy. Reaves went to Marks, as he had many times before, to set up a consignment so that he might invest some of his own money. Reaves, unlike other participants referred to in *Mr. Nice*, asked Marks to put him in direct contact with his exportation contacts rather than set the deal up for him. He used trust and security concerns as justification for direct access to such highly sought-after contacts. First, Reaves aimed for Marks' Pakistan exporter, Malik (N40). He then inquired about reaching Moynihan (N51), one of Marks' later contacts who maintained strong relations with politicians and smugglers in various countries in southeast Asia. Finally, Reaves succeeded in making direct contact with Marks' long-time associate, Jim McCann (N23). Marks' reaction to what was to follow proved less understanding – but still forgiving – than to the V11 incident: 'Roger had given Jim the £50,000 he required. Jim was ready to deliver. I felt a bit disgruntled about the two of them just carrying on as if I didn't exist, but I certainly didn't want to get in the way' (p. 329).

These two incidents are not the only examples of how Marks was leaving his rich social capital resources open to others and allowing his crucial brokerage position to be bypassed. He was giving away the competitive edge that had allowed him to endure and thrive in the trade; he was in the process of becoming redundant for some of his key contacts in precisely the same manner that Plinston had become redundant for him in the early 1970s.[4] This pattern emerges when one

---

4 Although this analysis assumes that Marks was unintentionally losing his competitive edge, Eddy and Walden (1991), who provide an account of Marks' fall, indicate that Marks was well aware of, indeed courted, operational redundancy: '"Just a couple of more years," he'd told Judy [Marks' wife]. His intention, he said, was to back out of the dope business gradually by acting only as a middleman, bringing

considers fluctuations in the structural hole content throughout his network.

Outcomes

Logged weights (in kilograms) per smuggling consignment serve as the principal outcome variable in this study. Total weight indicators, as already pointed out in Chapter 6, were excellent proxies for the less complete percentage-cut or profit measures. These specific activity outcomes were merged in three separate groups to account for Marks' movement in the cannabis trade. These phases constitute career outcomes in themselves. Relations between observed size (number of contacts), effective size, and network efficiency and the two set of outcomes proved telling in fitting a model to Marks' overall career and activities.

The three separate phases highlight the principal transitions (building, attainment, and fall) throughout Marks' career in and around importation segments of the cannabis trade. The forty-one consignments in Figure 4.3 were regrouped in the following manner: the building phase groups consignments 1 to 15; the attainment phase groups consignment 16 to 30; and the last return or 'fall' phase is represented by consignments 31 to 41 that were executed after Marks' release from prison in 1982. Means for each of Burt's structural hole indicators were subsequently calculated for each phase.

Figure 4.4 illustrates the patterns extending from these brokerage measures for the three phases across Marks' career. Results show that the building phase had Marks in direct working contact with the most co-participants (an average of almost five contacts per consignment), at his least effective (approximately two non-redundant contacts) and therefore at his least efficient (a low 39.7 per cent). Although his brokering seems somewhat inferior to that in the two later phases of his career, it must be noted that during this phase, in which he was building his network as a within-link importation coordinator, he was not operating with the same sizable shipments as he later would. Also, he was not yet a recognized player in the trade, nor was he an obvious target for law enforcement agents.

---

together suppliers and distributors. They would pay him a commission at first, but after a couple of deals they wouldn't need him any more and he'd be cut out – whatever the promises they made. It was his way of making himself redundant, eventually' (p. 222).

Figure 4.4 Marks' Personal Network Transitions by Career Phase

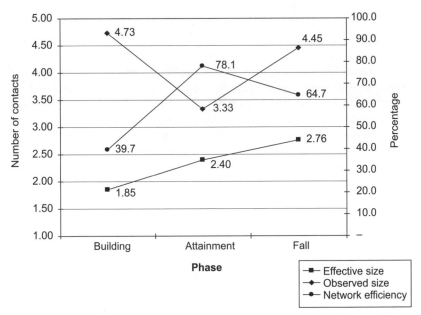

The term 'attainment phase' seems rightly coined. Marks, while main-taining, on average, direct contact with the least number of co-partici-pants per consignment (3.33; recall also the drop in his cumulative working network during this period, Figure 4.2), was more effective (2.4 contacts), and at his most efficient in filling his consignment-based networks with non-redundant contacts. For those consignments located during this phase of positional privilege, Marks averaged an efficiency rate of 78 per cent non-redundant contacts per all direct contacts, a considerable increase over the approximate 40 per cent that he aver-aged during his building phase. Fitting himself between links in the trade increased his efficiency and decreased his exposure to other co-participants. If we also take into consideration that, at this point, his trade activities were at their most stable (as indicated in Figure 4.3 and discussed earlier), with steady ventures offering repeated shipments and consistent profits from one-ton loads, it becomes clear that the late seventies in Marks' career were his busiest and most successful.

His return to the trade in 1983, although increasing the average effective size of his consignment networks (to 2.76 in Figure 4.4), also had him dealing directly with a slightly higher number of co-participants (observed size = 4.5). We have already seen in Figure 4.2 that Marks re-opened his network during this phase while continuing to fill the privileged between-link position. While he successfully closed his network during the attainment phase and therefore decreased the risks that come with increasing exposure, he was no longer practicing the same relational strategies in this return phase. The increase in observed size resulted in a decrease in his brokerage strategy as indicated by the drop in network efficiency (64.7 per cent). Marks re-opened his network, but unlike in his early years (the building phase), his reputation within the trade (in popular venues and among law enforcement officials) was no longer as discreet and low key. It was therefore more necessary for his actions to be properly insulated. He had attained the status of a public figure with the publication of one book on his career and the media circus surrounding his past arrests, trials, and subsequent incarceration. He had been released from prison just one year before this return to the trade. Such celebrity status and past reputation within law enforcement circles made him an obvious target for surveillance. Throughout many smuggling episodes during this last phase, it was evident that Marks and many of his co-participants were increasingly under the surveillance of DEA officials stationed in various cities throughout the world.

This non-linear trend (up, peak, and drop) representing the flow of Marks' networking throughout his career also emerges when we analyse the relation between individual consignment weights and relational indicators. Correlation results between logged weights and observed size for each smuggling network assembled for the forty-one consignments proved strong and positive ($r = 0.408$; $\alpha < .01$). This finding may seem obvious in that larger consignments do call for larger networks to be mobilized. That Marks was, himself, in direct contact with increasingly more people (the observed size of his network), however, is less obvious and was, as the phase transition analysis demonstrated, an indication of his own operating from one stage of his career to the next.

Similarly, the number of non-redundant contacts (effective size) across consignments also varied in a strong positive relation with the size of consignments ($r = 0.590$; $\alpha < .001$). In legitimate network terms, bigger is better (Burt 1992), but as already pointed out, privileged positioning brings with it greater efficiency – that is, by having the most proportionally non-redundant network possible. From this level of analysis, the number of non-redundant contacts remains closely related to the ob-

Figure 4.5 Marks' Network Efficiency by Size of Consignment

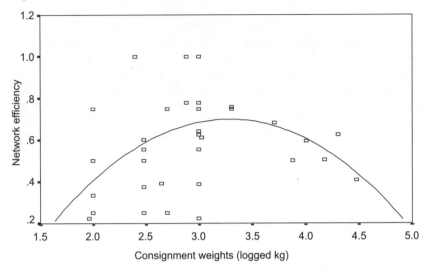

served size of a working network ($r = 0.599$; $\alpha < .001$). However, this does not entail that more non-redundant contacts through larger networks results in higher efficiency. This is demonstrated in applying a quadratic fit (see Figure 4.5) between network efficiency and logged weights ($r = 0.44$; $\alpha < .05$), which improves considerably on the linear model ($r = 0.17$; n.s.) and remains consistent with the non-linearity of the career phase outcomes discussed previously and illustrated with the network efficiency trend in Figure 4.4.

The pattern in Figure 4.5 establishes the initial increase and subsequent dampening-off of network efficiency in relation to consignment weights. Marks was at his most efficient when dealing with one thousand to about three thousand kilogram (between 3 and 3.5 logged kilogram) shipments. Although he had the personal network in place to receive offers to participate in multi-ton consignments, a downward trend was observed beyond the 3.5 logged kilogram point (more than three tons), illustrating that he was decreasingly efficient as a broker and therefore losing his competitive edge in comparison with consignments dealing with more personally optimally sized one-ton shipments. This results in decreasing returns for increasing network efficiency.

Limits are therefore evident in regard to Marks' own brokerage strategies. These limits appear to correspond with upper boundaries in the size of the tasks he chose to undertake. It also remains true (from previous observations in Figure 4.3) that the decreasingly inefficient brokered series of multi-ton consignments (the downward trend) took place in Marks' return to the trade after 1983.

The combination of increasing exposure within his personal network, decreasing efficiency while operating, increases in the size and amplitude of each consignment, and the obvious potential to be a prime target of external regulatory agents provide the circumstances that led to his ultimate downfall. Overall, the structural hole measures illustrate how Marks' cannabis trade ventures throughout his career (individual event outcomes) and the transitions between each (aggregate level outcomes) were structured by his personal working network and his own positioning within.

Accounting for Risks and Insulation

While the information extractable from *Mr. Nice* did not offer any suitable indicators of the level of surveillance targeting Marks from one phase or consignment to the next, we can nevertheless marshall evidence that Marks' most successful and network-efficient period was also the period in which he was the least likely to be targeted. Marks was a fugitive during the entire six-year attainment phase of his career (1975–80). Any form of physical detection would presumably have led to his arrest and subsequent trial for the smuggling charges laid in 1974, whether or not he was engaged in smuggling at that time. The name 'Howard Marks' thus did not figure in any transaction throughout these years; 'Donald Nice' was his principal alias during this period. Because he lasted for over six years as a fugitive under another identity, we may assume that he was not physically targeted, and this provides some evidence for the level of insulation he maintained during his smuggling ventures throughout this period. A plausible assertion extending from this finding accentuates the likely positive relationships between network closure, network efficiency, and insulation from external regulatory agents. This, of course, assumes that the player has the relational capacity and privilege to practice network closure while remaining operationally efficient.

The Independent Criminal Entrepreneur

Analysis of the information extracted from this autobiographical source shows that Marks was not the puppeteer of any criminal organization. This aspect of Marks' experience as an independent entrepreneur is reiterated within a recent study by Desroches (2005), who conducted seventy interviews with high-level drug traffickers. The experiences reported by these illegal drug merchants highlight the autonomy, improvisation, and flexibility that such entrepreneurs display in creating partnerships and working groups from one venture to the next. Marks was a highly resourceful player who fit in well with the needs and wants of other individuals or groups in the trade. He also seized and accumulated one entrepreneurial opportunity after another until he himself became the entrepreneurial opportunity to be seized by others looking to get ahead. Focusing on the brokerage position amongst criminal entrepreneurs illustrates how in business contexts in which non-contractual transactions and relations prevail, and the consequences of product illegality (Reuter 1983) are continuous obstacles to any player's livelihood and durability in the illegal trade, one's ability to reliably, consistently, and conveniently fit between other participants offers a more privileged *position* than that of an authoritarian *role* in any formal organization.

Marks' privileged status came more from his resourcefulness than from his ability to directly control the actions of others within a common organization. More specifically, Marks' ability to mobilize drug-smuggling assignments for others and serve as a network vector between key suppliers and buyers in early links of several cannabis trade chains led him to play the brokerage position within a specified network of participants to an increasingly greater extent. A distinction must therefore be made between 'international trader' and 'transnational boss' (Van Duyne 1996: p. 373) – the former Marks was, the latter he was not.

Whether Marks' form of 'flexible opportunism' or 'robust action' is atypical for a criminal entrepreneur remains a question on its own. Past researchers have found evidence of intermediaries and middlemen in drug trade settings (Reuter and Haaga 1989; Dorn, Murji, and South 1992; Adler 1993; Dorn, Oette, and White 1998), but this position has been largely left in the shadows of more conventional exporter, importer, wholesaler, or retailer categories. Brokers have been identified in these past studies, but they have yet to be fully assessed, and there have been few attempts to investigate this pivotal position within distribution chains of various illegal commodities. Deeper consideration of the broker in illegal trades shows, however, that although those trade participants occupying this position are clearly not controlling the chain or a given link in any formal authoritarian way, they are pivotal players for many buyers and sellers and therefore for the overall informal circulation process.

Interestingly, some of the most revealing insights on intermediaries in illegal trades extends from analyses of traditional forms of organized crime, and particularly of Sicilian and American versions of the Mafia (or Cosa Nostra). Whether as power brokers (Blok 1974), arbitrators of illegal market disputes (Reuter 1983), or suppliers of protection (Gambetta 1993), the middling roles and positions of Sicilian and North American Mafia-based entrepreneurs have been consistently proposed as valid concepts. One principal difference, however, between Mafia-linked brokerage and Marks' own brand is the apparent dependence on violence (or the threat of violence) in the former and its irrelevance in the latter.

It has been argued that the threat or use of violence is the obvious mechanism regulating competition in illegal trades (Schelling 1984). Burt's structural hole argument offers an alternative way of framing competition – that is, from a more cooperative angle. Marks' career provides evidence that it is possible to persist and succeed in criminal forms of enterprise without having to rely on instrumental violence. Structuring one's personal working network to include trade members who are not directly connected to each other but who may have inter-ests in dealing with one another represents a cooperative way of being competitive. The combination of reputation, know-how, consistent and quick access to privileged information sources, and non-redundant personal networking gives a player the competitive edge needed for further advancement. Whether many others have been able to endure for several years in criminal enterprise without experiencing the vio-lence typically associated with this line of work is another issue; it remains clear that our preconceptions of organized crime often have us following the thread of violence to begin with.

Marks himself notes that violence became increasingly apparent in his chosen field:

> The money we had made tended to dwarf that made by robbers, fraudsters, and thieves ... Accordingly, many heavy criminals had begun to deal dope, all kinds from anywhere. Some of the results were predictable. A lot more ruthlessness and violence was injected into dope-trading activity. Rip-offs and guns became more common. (p. 181)

The question whether instrumental violence in an illegal trade is a consequence of prolonged prohibition or the natural inclinations of criminal entrepreneurs themselves is partially settled by observing that non-violent cannabis smuggling, as documented by Marks, preceded violent cannabis smuggling. Violence is not an attractive instrument, nor is it a prudent course compared with other alternatives. Arlacchi (1988) elaborates on the interplay between trust and violence that is intrinsic in illegal drug trades. Trust is the initial contractual force. This force is entrenched within a player's or group's relational strength in a segment of the trade. Violence is the long-term sanctioning reaction for regulating disrespected informal contracts, not a proactive mechanism for personal advancement. The 'rip-off,' in this sense, precedes the 'gun.' A trade or market setting that was initially structured on trust, loyalty, and therefore network fundamentals may, after repeated resorts to violence to sanction uncooperative players, evolve into a setting designed around coercive and fraudulent methods of domination (p. 40).

In a case study of a career organized crime participant in Italy, Cottino (1998) also found that killing was a final recourse (p. 107). Similarly, Gambetta (1988) has discussed the limits of violence within the context of the Mafia in southern Italy. 'Violence by itself,' writes Gambetta, 'will not do. It is risky, costly, and generates instability and conflict: explaining the persistence of the Mafia simply by its capacity for coercion would be nearly as limited as explaining the persistence of capitalism on the same basis' (p. 170). The author argues in favour of understanding other, 'more powerful' weapons to promote cooperation and assure group survival – chief among them the mutual satisfaction of economic interests.

Trust and relational mechanisms precede the development of violence. Mutual aid precedes outright regulatory competition. Within such a framework, instrumental violence becomes a supplementary or back-up resource used when one's overall relational force within a prohibited transactional setting proves insufficient in assuring proper working protocol between co-participants. The matter, however, does warrant additional research in contexts where violence is obvious and visible.

5 Career Opportunities in the Cosa Nostra

In December 1990, the FBI terminated a decade of surveillance that targeted one of the key Cosa Nostra units in New York City. The arrests of the Gambino family administration – boss John Gotti, underboss Salvatore Gravano, and consigliere Frank Locascio – led to a series of turnabouts resulting from Gravano's decision, in October 1991, to become an FBI informant.

Gravano provided evidence that led to the eventual conviction of Gotti and Locascio. Both received life sentences without parole. Gravano also attested to his own participation in nineteen murders as well as a wide array of other criminal activities throughout his twenty-five-year career within the ranks of the Cosa Nostra. In exchange for this ensemble of information, Gravano pleaded guilty to a single count of racketeering with a maximum twenty-year sentence; all other charges were dropped. With the backing of several law enforcement officials who prepared written referrals vouching for his value, courage, and truthfulness (Capeci and Mustain 1996: p. 444), Gravano received, in September 1994, a five-year sentence and a three-year supervised release to follow. Since the five-year term incorporated the four previous years during which he had been detained while serving as an informant, he actually served only one more year in prison.

Gravano's confessions of the series of murder plots in which he was implicated had many pointing the finger at his capacity for violence as the key factor accounting for his advancement in the Cosa Nostra. Gravano was certainly both violent and successful in his ways. A capacity for violence may seem to explain his success, but a closer analysis of the non-violent aspects of his career allows us to develop an alternative framework explaining his progression within the ranks of the Gambino family.

Jacobs (1999), in his study of Cosa Nostra legitimate industry infiltration in New York City preceding the crackdown that took place during the 1980s, provided the following account of Gravano's career:

> The career of Gambino underboss Sammy 'The Bull' Gravano provides an excellent example of the energy, imagination, and entrepreneurship that characterize the Italian American organized crime families. Sammy Gravano, a man with only a grade-school education, made millions of dollars in legitimate businesses. He was a consummate mobster-entrepreneur: energetic, imaginative, and resourceful. He advanced from small-time hustler to owner of nightclubs and plumbing, drywall, carpeting, and painting companies. Ultimately, Gravano acquired interests in several parts of the construction industry: concrete pouring, asbestos, floor-inlay, and steel-erection companies. His status in the mob enabled him to carry out contracts and guarantee labor peace to cooperative subcontractors, who repaid the favor with kickbacks ranging from $15,000 to $20,000 per contract. In 1989, he handed over close to $1.2 million in profits from rigged construction bids to Gambino family crime boss John Gotti. Gravano, like many of the Cosa Nostra figures, kept seeking opportunities to make money in one business scheme and racket after another. He capitalized on his reputation as a Cosa Nostra member and on the network of connections that Cosa Nostra membership provided him. In addition, and like many of his underworld colleagues, his outgoing, even charismatic, personality was an asset in dealing with business people who apparently concluded that Gravano was no mobster, but an 'underworld' figure who shared their passion for business. (p. 119)

Viewing a mafioso in an entrepreneurial context is not novel in research. Arlacchi (1983), for example, made this link in demonstrating the innovative and capitalistic character that became the Sicilian Mafia's ideal during the 1970s:

> For the most articulate *mafiosi*, the adoption of modern capitalist values is expressed in terms of a religion of accumulation whose seriousness should not be underestimated: profit and power are regarded, not as a means to the satisfaction of material needs, but as the goals of life ... Profit and power denote that the *mafioso* is an able exponent of his 'profession', and this ability is the alpha and omega of his moral universe. (pp. 119–20)

Like the independent Marks (see Chapter 4), Gravano was relationally proficient, and it was through opportunities extending from his personal network of working contacts that he was able to climb the promotional ladder within the Gambino family, expanding his business ventures and financial yields as a racketeer and increasingly legitimate construction entrepreneur. To understand the place of (lethal) violence in Gravano's career, we must first situate this career within the social network process that was more generally at the root of his advancement as a criminal entrepreneur.

The Career Working Network

Figure 5.1 presents the sixty-eight nodes (Gravano plus sixty-seven contacts) that made up Gravano's core working network from his early street-gang years during the late 1950s in Bensonhurst, Brooklyn, to his December 1990 arrest and ultimate career fall within the Cosa Nostra. Gravano is assigned ego status and is indicated as Node 1 (N1). Each contact (all are male and most are of Italian descent) is identified by the date he entered Gravano's working network. Of the sixty-seven, thirty-five were documented as having become official (made) members in various family units in New York City (all thirty-five made members are underlined in Figure 5.1). Of these thirty-five, twenty-seven were members of the Gambino family. As Gravano's career progressed, his network became increasingly filled with such made members.

Network Channels and Concentrated Contact Allotment

A pattern of contact entrance across distinct phases in Gravano's career can be observed in Figure 5.1. Contacts enter in clusters that correspond to the time periods denoting Gravano's promotions within the Cosa Nostra. Each time period is also marked by a central contact. These promotions and central contacts intertwine to offer him access to new opportunities that are attained through and realized with others. New opportunities are therefore made concrete by the contacts that offer and help effectuate them. The centralized clustering pattern that emerges from Figure 5.1 marks the concentrated manner in which contacts and business resources were allotted to Gravano throughout the building stages of his career.

Each phase or cluster is constructed through one person in the previous phase. The N2 to N8 ensemble, for example, represents Gravano's

Figure 5.1 Gravano's Career Working Network

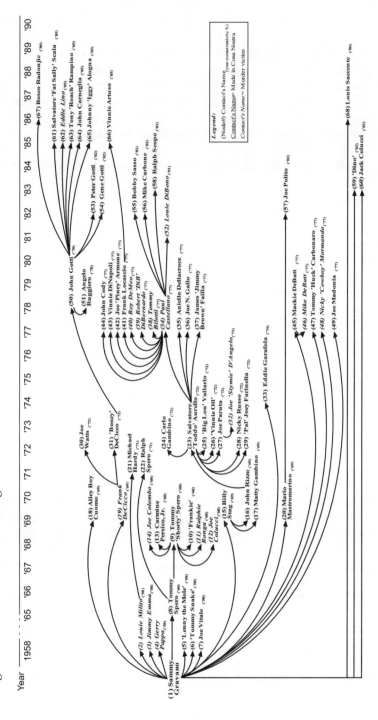

years as a member of a juvenile gang (the Rampers). In 1968, N8 connected Gravano to his uncle, N9, who later initiated Gravano's entrance and association within the Colombo family (N9 to N14). Gravano remained associated with the Colombo family until 1972, when a conflict arose with N9's brother, N22. The resolution of this conflict resulted in his transfer to the Gambino family through the aid of N16, who allowed Gravano to connect with and move under the supervision of a Gambino captain, N23. Throughout the following years, N23 ('Toddo' Aurello) became Gravano's mentor, tutor, supervisor, and initial sponsor within that family.

This marked the onset of his long-term affiliation with the Gambinos. Immediate contacts were made through N23 with the working crew (N25 to N29) that Gravano would be a part of for various criminal activities. Contact was also made with Carlo Gambino (N24), the family boss, but Gambino exerted little influence within Gravano's own career. In 1977, N23 sponsored Gravano to be made an official Gambino soldier. N23 also gave Gravano access to a wide network of new contacts, and therefore new opportunities within the family, by connecting him with four key Gambino members (N34 to N37).

By officially entering the family and connecting with the new family boss (N34, Paul Castellano) through N23, Gravano succeeded in gaining direct access to Gambino resources (namely, N38 to N44; N43 and N44 were part of N34's personal social capital who were well positioned within contracting and labour sectors in New York City's construction industry). N38 and N39 were key Gambino construction entrepreneurs or racketeers, as was another Gambino member (N19) with whom Gravano had been acquainted since 1969. The remainder of the contacts who entered Gravano's network in 1977 through N34 would become more influential to Gravano's venturing and advancement somewhat later in his career. Aside from these immediate contacts that Gravano accessed through N34 in 1977, four others (all linked to the construction industry: N52, N55, N56, and N58) entered his network during the early eighties through N34. This established Gravano's full transition to construction racketeer and increasing detachment as a street gangster/bandit and small-business scammer.

The N23–N34 channel of connections structured Gravano's movement from Gambino associate to soldier to construction racketeer. At this point, Gravano branched out on his own and sought out new opportunities. One of these came through his link with N50 (John Gotti), who was, at that time (1978), also an official member of another faction (crew) within the family. N50 became an acquaintance of Gravano through an informal introduction made by N31 in 1978. N31's place within Gravano's working network is justified only by this one, crucial, introduction.

The remaining contacts in Figure 5.1 represent those made by Gravano himself (or ones for whom I was not able to identify the actual contact provider) or by individuals who proved useful for certain events/ transitions but remained minor figures throughout his career. For example, the main channel in Gravano's personal working network (N23–N34) was triggered by his contact with N15 – a minor figure in his career but key during 1969 in making Gravano aware of an opportunity to participate in a Brooklyn after-hours club venture. This connection led to an immediate link with N16, who would later connect Gravano to likely the most important figure throughout his career: N23. N23 would later connect Gravano to N34, who would provide him access to the elite within the Cosa Nostra.

A secondary network channel triggered by an early relation with another eventual Gambino strongman, N19, led to the subsequent connection to N50, which would create an alternative channel useful in overcoming a break-up in the major N23–N34 vein. No significant contacts were documented as entering Gravano's personal working network after 1986.

Overall, contact allotment in Gravano's career is concentrated amongst four key contacts who combined to contribute 52 per cent of his working network (five contacts or 7.5 per cent from N9; ten contacts or 14.9 per cent from N23; eleven contacts or 16.4 per cent from N34; and nine contacts or 13.3 per cent from N50). Each of these four contacts marked pivotal transitions in Gravano's career. N9 brought Gravano out of the street gang and into the Cosa Nostra; N23 was Gravano's maker in the Gambino family; N34 was his link to the family elite and the construction industry; and N50 was the connection that allowed Gravano to independently go beyond the resources formerly made available by the gatekeeper N34.

Network Dynamics and Event/Phase Associations

All contacts in Figure 5.1 were traced for their years of entrance and exit in Gravano's network. This established the cumulative working network (see Figure 5.2). Entering contacts are added to the sum of contacts already in place for the previous year, while exiting contacts are

Figure 5.2 Gravano's Career Representation

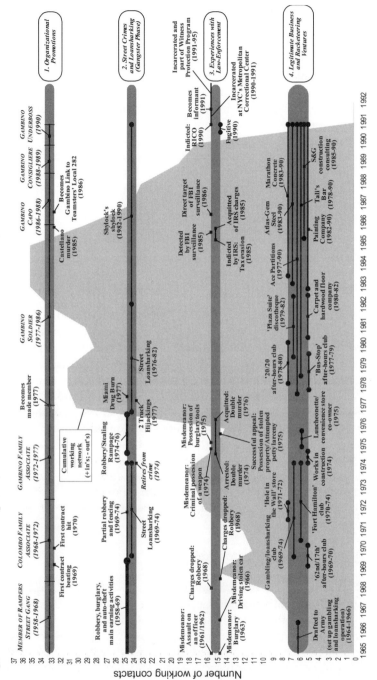

subtracted from that annual total. For example, Gravano began with six contacts in 1965, added another contact (one in, zero out) in 1966, remained stable at seven contacts for 1967, and increased to nine (six in, four out) in 1968. The cumulative distribution collapses in 1990–1 after Gravano was arrested by the FBI and defected from the Cosa Nostra to become a government informant.

The ensemble of the cumulative working network and the superimposed event/activity axes in Figure 5.2 provides a representation of Gravano's career as an organizationally bounded criminal entrepreneur. It also allows us to focus on associations between network dynamics and experiences throughout this career. The following section presents the links between key relational qualities and event/activities across various phases (onset, early building, advanced building, attainment) in Gravano's career.

Pre–Cosa Nostra Experiences

From as early as 1958 (when he was thirteen years of age), Gravano was connected to one of the many juvenile street gangs (the Rampers) active in the Bensonhurst district of Brooklyn. Fighting, robbing, and stealing were the main activities during his years with the Rampers. Gravano dropped out of school at sixteen, after which he became fully engaged in the same criminal activities he had already been implicated in. This phase lasted until he was drafted into the army in 1964. For the next two years, Gravano fulfilled his draft duties while finding time, within the confines of his military training, for his first gambling and loan-sharking operations. In 1966, he was honourably discharged from the army and returned to Bensonhurst, where he reconnected with the Rampers and their expanding activities. By 1968 (when Gravano was twenty-three), the limits of street-gang affiliation were becoming apparent; he sought new opportunities.

Early Building Phase (Apprenticeship)

The building phase in Gravano's career as a criminal entrepreneur began with his entrance into Cosa Nostra working circles. This transition took place through one of his fellow Ramper members (N8 in Figure 5.1), who connected Gravano to his uncle (N9), who was affiliated to one of the five established Cosa Nostra unities in New York City (the Colombo family). Gravano recalled this recruitment as follows:

His [N9's] message wasn't anything I hadn't heard before. Eventually, I'd have to hook up with the right people. But the way he put it was different. 'I've had my eye on you,' he says. 'Why not come with me? You're a tough guy, but you can't keep doing things your own way. You can't live your whole life on your own. Sooner or later, you're going to get in real trouble or get killed. I'll give you a different relationship, where you can be somebody. (Maas 1997: p. 35)

During these early years as a Colombo and later Gambino associate, Gravano continued primarily to be active in street crimes (robbery, burglary, auto-theft, fencing). Figure 5.2 points out that he also became an active street-level loan shark[1] soon after he associated himself with the Colombo family (see Axis 2).

Axis 3 in Figure 5.2 shows us that Gravano had been successful during his street-gang years in having potential felonies plea-bargained down to misdemeanours – 'I don't mind taking a plea, because misdemeanors really don't count. It's felonies that screw up your life' (p. 23). Connecting with the Cosa Nostra unity allowed him to be more proactive in his earning activities and also more suitably reactive or resistant to confrontations with law enforcement. His affiliation with the Colombo family offered the added resource of extended connections that likely allowed the judicial process to be avoided altogether. In two robbery incidents, Gravano was arrested and faced witness-backed prosecutions. In both cases, witnesses were dealt with through the Colombo family's extended connections. For the first robbery, Gravano explained:

It turns out the guy, the owner of the store, is a friend of a made guy in Sam the Plumber's family – the DeCalvacante family – over in Jersey. Shorty [N9], whoever, gets in touch with him and he talks to the owner. It was all set up the next time I was in court. The owner walks in and goes in front of the judge and says, 'Your Honor, I picked the defendant out from this picture, but now that I see him in person, that's not him.' And the case is thrown out. (p. 36)

For the second robbery accusation, Gravano provided the following account: 'Sure enough, we find out one of the guards made me. And the

---

1 Gravano distinguished between street-level loan sharking (lending 'ninety-six for a hundred-twenty for twelve weeks ... to the bottom of the barrel' [Maas 1997: p. 41]) and the upgraded 'Shylock's Shylock' that he would become by the early eighties.

cops are looking to arrest me. But guess what? The guard knows Carmine Persico's [N13] cousin and is a little crooked himself. The guard reaches out and says for ten thousand he ain't going to see nothing. He won't testify' (p. 38).

Gravano's promotional axis (Axis 1) in Figure 5.2 indicates that his first contractual assignments were also conducted during his Colombo association. One way for legitimate organizational members to better their chances of promotion is to take part in high-profile assignments (Burt 1992: p. 127). Contract beatings and murder are such assignments in Cosa Nostra–like unities. For the former, Gravano was assigned to beat up, and return with the ear of, a man who had been in conflict with N13's brother. Gravano executed the order and reported back to N13 without the man's ear, but with news that he had succeeded in completely knocking off his little finger with a blackjack. The high-ranking N13 proved satisfied with Gravano's accomplishment (p. 46).

The change in his organizational profile after his first contract murder in 1970 was similarly well received:

> I would say that this was my stepping-stone in the mob. I mean, after the hit ... Rumor had it that we – Shorty's crew – had done work and that Sammy the Bull was the workhorse in the crew. So I wasn't waiting on lines no more. I wasn't just another tough guy on the street. I was getting a different kind of respect and so on and so forth. The word was that I ranked high with Carmine Persico [N13] and they had the intention someday after the books were open that Sammy was going to be made. (p. 53)

Connecting with the Colombo family also gave Gravano his initial opportunities to start his own (quasi-)legitimate businesses (see Axis 4 in Figure 5.2) and decrease his higher risk street-crime activities: 'Even if they're not stone legitimate businesses, they're real on a business level' (p. 39). One of these business ventures led to the conflict that had him transferred to the Gambino family in 1972.

Between his association with the Gambino family in 1972 and his official entrance in 1977, Gravano remained under the strict tutelage of N23. Under N23's supervision, Gravano's network increased slightly during the first years (from twelve contacts in 1971 to eighteen in 1974). This gradual rise may be accounted for by the fellow crew members allocated and supervised by N23.

A drop, however, takes place in his criminal working network at the moment that he decided to retire from crime (see Axis 2 in Figure 5.2) for the first and only time in his career. Gravano, until that point, had remained largely active in the same street crimes and low-level loan sharking activities. He had also continued to involve himself in various after-hour and gambling clubs (Axis 4). He made little progress in regard to his criminal earnings. In 1974, he held two consecutive legitimate jobs as a construction labourer. While he remained in contact with N23, Gravano relied on such legitimate work for about one year.

This legitimate phase in Gravano's career came to an end with his arrest and indictment on a double-murder charge (along with N18 in Figure 5.1) in late 1974. While out on bail for these murder charges and faced with heavy legal fees and debts to N23 (and others within the Gambino family), Gravano quit his legitimate construction job and embarked on a roughly year-and-a-half robbery and stealing spree with N18: 'I had to go back to Brooklyn. ... There's no way I could work for two fifty with the expenses I got now .... To pay the lawyer, to pay back Toddo [N23] – that ten thousand sounds like nothing now, but it was a lot then – I'm out every single night, seven days a week, robbing and stealing with Alley Boy [N18]' (p. 78).

The combination of his decision to go straight, the subsequent murder charges that brought him back into crime, and the intensively high-risk street-crime spree accounts for the slight drop in his cumulative working network between 1974 and 1976 (from eighteen to fourteen contacts). During this period Gravano also faced three other criminal charges, of which two were plea-bargained to misdemeanours and one was successfully appealed (see Axis 3 between 1974 and 1976). In addition to the street-crime spree, he also operated a convenience store and luncheonette with N18 in order to supplement his earnings and pay back his growing debts extending from his judicial situation.

Figure 5.2 (Axis 3) shows that this double-murder charge was finally dropped in 1976, but Gravano maintains that this event sealed his working affiliation to crime and the Cosa Nostra:

That pinch changed my whole life. I never, ever stopped a second from there on in. I was like a madman. Never stopped stealing. Never stopped robbing. I was obsessed. I had been looking to pull away, going out to Long Island with my wife, raising a family, going to work and maybe going into my own business as soon as I got on my feet a little bit. Maybe it wasn't meant to be. But that Dunn brothers thing [the double-murder charge] glued me to the mob, that's for shit sure. And then Toddo Aurello [N23] proposed me to be made in the Gambino family. So that was it. (p. 80)

Advanced Building Phase (Being Made)

The key transition of being made (becoming an official member of or accepted insider in the family) in 1977 (see Axis 1 in Figure 5.2) is marked by a sharp rise in Gravano's cumulative network (from fourteen in 1976 to thirty in 1977). While he had been able to access various Cosa Nostra resources as an associate, these resources were largely limited to whatever was made available through his supervisor, N23. As a soldier in the family, Gravano was able to expand beyond N23's personal resources. He was now inside the organization and in a position to explore a wide array of business opportunities that branched out beyond that organization.

Soon after Gravano was made, his street-crime activities faded away (see Axis 2). Aside from a few robbery incidents in 1977, loan-sharking was the only activity that continued from his pre-soldier period. No other street crimes were documented in his biography after 1977. Similarly, no confrontations with law enforcement agents were found for several years after he was made (Axis 3). Instead, he considerably increased his legitimate or racketeering ventures (Axis 4). Gravano began his first construction company in 1977 (Ace Partitions), opened two after-hour clubs (Bus Stop and 20/20) around the same time, and established his personal Bensonhurst headquarters (Tali's Bar) around 1978. Aside from another venture with a Brooklyn discotheque (Plaza Suite) in 1979, all other businesses appearing along Axis 4 were oriented towards the construction industry.

How was his entrance and increasing involvement in New York City's construction industry linked to his rise in the Cosa Nostra? First, one must accentuate the role of the family unit in providing the made member with improved opportunities to accumulate various forms of capital. Becoming a soldier meant that Gravano was allowed to set up his own personal links with associates looking to improve their status with Cosa Nostra members. Such associates had their own (legitimate or criminal) businesses and activities in operation and, as Gravano had done and continued to do with his own sponsor, N23, were required to mete out portions of their earnings to their supervisors. This upward allocation of earnings allows higher ranked members to supplement the revenues from their own ventures with the cuts contributed by their underlings. This supplement, which varies with the financial achievements of the ensemble of contributing underlings, allows accumulation of financial capital to increase as rank within the family increases. The higher one is in this vertical distribution scheme, the more likely one is to have a receiving hand in a wider array of profits from other members and associates. For Gravano, the promotion to soldier allowed him to supplement his personal earnings (profits from clubs and loan sharking) with those of his new associates. His expanding social capital allowed him to accumulate enough financial capital to begin his own construction company.

In starting his first construction company (plumbing and drywall) with his brother-in-law (N33), he attracted the interest of the Gambino family boss, N34. This established the second relational feature of Gravano's rise in New York City's construction industry. With N34's support, Gravano came to realize the utility of such contacts within legitimate industries. He recalled N34 assuring him: 'You need entree into the unions, the contractors, anybody, you let me know. We know them all. I'll help you.' Gravano added: 'And he did. The better I did, the better it is for the borgata, the family' (p. 106).

It was through N34 and around this period that Gravano began the final segment of the building phase in his career. The cumulative working network in Figure 5.2 increases to a peak of thirty-five contacts in 1983. Between Gravano's official entrance into the Gambino family in 1977 and his full-time emergence in the construction industry in 1983, nine construction-based contacts were added to his network (N43, N44, N49, N55–N60). Six of the nine contacts were allocated by N34. In addition to these contacts, Gravano also established dealing relations (once again, through N34) with at least three other Gambino family members who were also active in various sectors of the construction industry (N38, N39, and N52). The increasing concentration of his earning activities in construction is particularly revealed between 1981 and 1983 in that seven of all nine contacts entering his network were construction-based contacts. In a time span of approximately six years, Gravano expanded his businesses into various areas of industrial construction: plumbing, drywall, carpet and hardwood floor installations, painting, steel erection, and concrete pouring.

While the place of the Cosa Nostra in Gravano's progression cannot be overlooked, it is important to emphasize his personal capacities as well. The Cosa Nostra offers the potential for its members to access better opportunities and therefore to advance their own careers, but this is not a given for all its members, nor does it typify the operations of the Cosa Nostra as a whole. Gravano successfully established himself in the construction industry because he succeeded in accessing rich resources through N34's and not necessarily the Gambino family's network: 'The more I was in construction, the more Paul [N34] got interested in me. He was helping me. He was watching to see what kind of a guy I really was business-wise. I guess he liked what he saw because he started calling me in more and more' (Maas 1997: p. 115). Not all members could be expected to have or want such access to opportunities for advancement. That Gravano did and that he subsequently expanded these opportunities is indicated by the drop following his network peak between 1983 and 1985.

Elite Membership

By 1985, Gravano was well positioned in a growing number of sectors in New York City's construction industry. Through N34, he had attained working relations with the consecutive presidents of Teamster Local 282 (N44 and later N55), the Gambino representative to this local (N39), the president for the Local District Council of the Cement and Concrete Workers Union (N58), and various subcontractors. A blend of costly labour tactics, contract arrangements, price-fixing, kickbacks, and good-quality work allowed Gravano to substantially increase his personal earnings and enhance his name in this legitimate industry.

Although there is little information available to accurately estimate his revenue throughout his transition from street criminal to construction racketeer, some of his personal investments point to an increase in wealth. Aside from the ever-expanding investments in a wide array of construction companies (Axis 4 in Figure 5.2), Gravano bought the Brooklyn discotheque Plaza Suite in 1979, which he sold in 1982 for the round sum of one million dollars. He was indicted by the IRS in 1985 (see Axis 3) for evading $300 000 in taxes from that sale. As Figure 5.2 illustrates, these IRS charges were dropped that same year. Gravano also purchased, at some point during the early eighties, a New Jersey thirty-acre ranch. The monetary amounts associated with these two investments and his continual expansion in the construction industry, although not providing exact figures on his earnings, do attest to an increasingly lucrative career.

These indications of achievement accompany the peak and drop in the size of his working network. His financial capital had reached a point at which he was able to cease searching for new contacts, thrive off the rich personal network that was already in place, and reduce the overall number of contacts that made up his working network. He also upgraded his criminal loan-sharking to that of a Shylock's Shylock status (see Axis 2). By the mid-eighties, his wealth was consistently on the rise and his business activities were expanding. Within the Gambino family, however, he remained a soldier and had not had a promotion in rank since officially entering the family unit in 1977. One key event, his direct participation in the assassination of the family boss (N34), would subsequently open up further promotional opportunities for Gravano.

The 'taking out' of N34 from his and other Gambino family members' working networks removed a once-necessary opportunity provider who had become, for Gravano and likely for others in the family, an obstacle to further career progression. Immediately after N34 was murdered, Gravano obtained a promotion to capo under the new Gambino boss, John Gotti (N50). Gravano and N50 had been acquainted since 1978, but their relationship really tightened throughout the first half of the eighties. The preparations surrounding the assassination of N34 served as the focus that brought them together on a more consistent basis. This association offered Gravano an avenue that went beyond the opportunities accessed through N34. It also led to his promotion to crew captain, or capo, positioning him within the elite core of the Gambino family.

The network closure trend found in the cumulative working network in Figure 5.2 began around the same period that Gravano was promoted to capo. The drop took place between 1985 and 1986 (from thirty-five to twenty-nine contacts) and continued until 1990 (twenty-four contacts in 1987, twenty-three in 1988, nineteen in 1989, and seventeen in 1990), the year that Gravano fell to the FBI task force that had been investigating and intensely monitoring him and several other Gambino family members. Figure 5.2 shows that Gravano was first detected by the FBI surveillance net in 1985 and became a direct target in 1986 (see Axis 3). The career representation also shows that he had not been arrested since the period preceding his official entrance as a soldier in the Gambino family.

As we saw with Marks' experience, closing one's network is a privilege and allows the criminal entrepreneur to remain selective in choosing opportunities. As a Gambino captain, Gravano was in the most entrepreneurial position of his career. At this rank, he was able to broker between at least three separate clusters of contacts: (1) his personal crew of soldiers; (2) the family administration; and (3) various legitimate partners with whom he was increasingly involved. His focus on the construction industry was further enhanced after he took on the crucial role of Gambino link to the Teamsters Local 282 in 1986 (see Axis 1), which gave him quasi-exclusive control of family members' interests in that industry:

> I had control of the whole thing. The president, who was Bobby Sasso [N55], the vice-president, the secretary/treasurer, delegates, foremen ... I said to report directly to me if he [N55] heard anything. From here on in he was to answer to me on the construction jobs. He wasn't to meet with anybody from any other family unless it was strictly union business. Anything else, any schemes they had, was to go through me or John Gotti [N50]. (p. 220)

Later Gravano further clarified his exclusive control of the family's construction interests, saying 'John [N50] didn't know anything about construction' (p. 230).

Gravano's personal network, as a capo, therefore spanned three fundamental holes. His promotion to capo allowed Gravano to reduce the number of new contacts entering his network. This is the privilege of well-positioned participants in an organized crime process: their ability to restrict the number of contacts involved in their illegal operations allows them to remain relatively insulated from prosecution. While their reputation and status increase amongst criminal participants and law enforcement targeters alike, their distance from the riskier segments of action in any venture makes them less vulnerable to effective prosecution, even as they remain at the centre of systematic forms of surveillance. Such shadow or brokering participants are the highly suspected yet difficult-to-catch players. These players have a hand, yet not necessarily control, in a wide array of illegal operations but are not directly implicated in the most visible and detectable segments of these activities. Gravano's control in the family, for example, was fully oriented towards legitimate operations.

The paradox of this position, as illustrated in Figure 5.2 (Axis 3), is that the criminal entrepreneur faces an increased possibility of being the target of surveillance but a decreased likelihood of arrest and subsequent prosecution. That the cumulative network drop persists throughout the following years and his later two promotions into the family's administration (to consigliere in 1988 and underboss in 1989), evidences the continuous exclusivity of Gravano's working network and embedded opportunities.

Promotional advancement within the Gambino family allowed Gravano to modify his earnings activities throughout his career, decreasing his involvement in street crimes and increasing his involvement in racketeering in legitimate business, as well as decreasing arrests and increasing the level of surveillance that he attracted. Figure 5.2 also demonstrates how such promotional transitions coincide with fluctuations in the cumulative count of Gravano's core working network throughout his career.

As noted above, this network explanation of organizational promotion has been more fully developed, albeit in legitimate contexts, in Burt's (1992) structural hole theory. Applying this theory and its operations to Gravano's career will allow us to further investigate the inner mechanisms that account for the promotion-network relation that has been found to be so crucial to success, resistance, adaptability (flexibility), and persistence in criminal forms of enterprise.

Network Properties and Organized Criminal Entrepreneurial Careers

Criminal professions call for participants to be able to adapt to highly constrained settings. This is especially true of organized criminal enterprise (orthodox organized crime) contexts. Such settings require the establishment of a continuous working or co-offending process. Attaining a privileged position requires an entrepreneur to distinguish himself from his co-participants and competitors. While not all organizationally bounded criminal entrepreneurs may follow the same processes Gravano went through during his career, it is clear that the model of his trajectory in the Cosa Nostra is helpful for understanding high levels of achievement in organized crime and other long-term criminal processes.

Promotion and Achievement

Achievement in a Cosa Nostra family is indicated by one's capacity to climb the promotional ranks within the unit. Understanding the likelihood of ascending within the family allows us to understand the task facing the criminal participant. Over a span of approximately thirteen years beginning with his official entrance into the family (in 1977), Gravano rose to underboss (second in command) within the Gambino family. Such advancement, as in legitimate contexts, is not a given, simply because a hierarchical structure offers few executive positions.

Reports on the structure of a typical Cosa Nostra family unit have remained consistent since Valachi's initial 1963 testimony (Maas 1968). Gravano's biography provides further confirmation of that structure as outlined in both North American and Sicilian Mafia/Cosa Nostra contexts by Cressey (1969), Albini (1971), Anderson (1979), Abadinsky (1983), and Arlacchi (1992, 1994). Aside from the three ranks at its administrative core (boss, underboss, and consigliere), Gravano identified twenty-two captains in the Gambino family.[2] A New York State Organized Crime Task Force, in a 1986 report (see Davis 1993: p. 291), revealed a similar estimate of twenty-three Gambino captains. Davis (1993) estimated each of the Gambino captain's crews to contain between twenty and twenty-five soldiers. The information provided by Gravano (in Maas 1997) revealed a much lower count: Gravano never seemed to be a part of or responsible for a crew that comprised more than ten soldiers. I will opt for this latter, more conservative estimate of ten soldiers over the Davis count of twenty. The number of associates remains difficult to estimate, as Davis's rough guess of 'several thousand' tells us (p. 291). Other estimates ranged from four to ten associates for each soldier (Jacobs 1999). Because of such discrepancies, here I will discuss only official ranks (soldier to boss).

With a maximum of four official ranks (soldier, captain, secondary administration, and boss), opportunities for promotion in the Cosa Nostra's Gambino family appear extremely limited. Other roles are available within the organization (e.g., union local representative, coordinator for a specific illegal activity)[3] but remain secondary to the made

---

2 This information was obtained from FBI debriefings available at the Smoking Gun website (15 November 1991): www.thesmokinggun.com/gravano/gravano19b.html.

3 Gravano gave little indication of the existence of official corrupter and enforcer roles as identified by Cressey (1969). It seemed that the need for corruption was specific to distinct activities. As regards killing or engaging in violent acts for the family, Gravano's accounts suggest that while some members are consistently involved in regulating within the organization, on a hit the shooter, orchestrator, and back-up members tend to vary. Everyone was expected to kill for the family (that was part of the membership oath), but no one was exclusively assigned this role. Gravano's explanation, however, does indicate that while the role was not assigned to any one member, contract killing was generally a group assignment and was taken care of by various crews.

ranks. Using the lower number provided by Gravano, I estimate that the Gambino family consisted of approximately 220 (10 × 22) soldiers,[4] 22 captains, 2 secondary administrators, and 1 boss.

If all other factors are held constant, the probability of advancement remains slim for any given official member. Each soldier has a one in ten chance of being promoted to captain.[5] Each captain faces a 9 per cent (2/22) chance of becoming either a consigliere or underboss. The long-term odds that a given soldier will enter this secondary administrative core[6] throughout his career are therefore approximately one in one hundred (0.9 per cent = 2/220 or 0.09 × 0.1).[7] These are the odds that Gravano beat. That he beat them constitutes his status as a successful organizationally affiliated criminal entrepreneur; how he beat them is our concern here.

Movements in an Organized Crime Career

The *early building* phase marked Gravano's years as a Colombo and Gambino associate. A more *advanced building* phase that saw Gravano move into more prosperous and secure activities began with his official attachment as a soldier in the Gambino family. After a lengthy period as a soldier, Gravano was promoted to capo. This established the *attainment* phase of his career, which would bring further promotions into and within the family administration as consigliere and underboss. These three phases highlight the critical shifts Gravano went through during his criminal entrepreneurial career.

As already demonstrated, these three general movements coincide with overall network transitions throughout his career. The following analysis will demonstrate, more specifically, how these movements are structured by constraint and hierarchical-constraint variations within the evolution of his overall networking.

Figure 5.3 reveals the cyclical progression of Gravano's career and provides further relational substance to the idea that rank, promotion, or organization are plausible components to some forms of crime. Both

---

4 Using Davis's (1993) higher count, the number of soldiers would increase to 440 (20 × 22).

5 Note, however, that the turnover – ins and outs – of individual crew membership is not accounted for here.

6 I assume that each soldier must first become a captain in order to have a chance to enter the administrative core.

7 Using Davis's (1993) estimates, each soldier would have a 0.45 per cent (2/440) chance of making it into the administration.

Figure 5.3 Gravano's Constraints and Hierarchical Constraints across Promotions

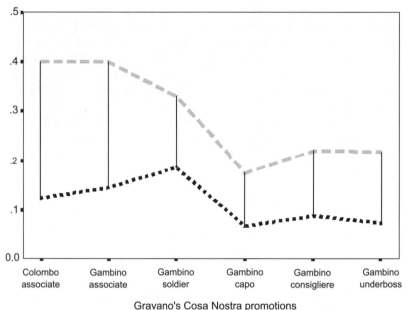

Gravano's Cosa Nostra promotions

Network constraints
Hierarchical constraints

network constraints (upper sequence) and hierarchical constraints (lower sequence) are plotted across promotional phases. Throughout the first two promotions (as a Colombo and Gambino associate), Gravano was at his most relationally constrained (C = 0.4 for both periods). He was also weakly positioned as an outsider (unofficial member) to each of the affiliated families, making him an unlikely candidate for strategic sponsorship by a high-ranked and entrepreneurially bent official member who would provide opportunities beyond those offered by his own supervisor (hierarchical constraints for Gravano's network during the Colombo and Gambino associate periods are, respectively, 0.12 and 0.15).

Once Gravano was made a soldier in the family and gained official access to established others, constraints decreased by 18 per cent (to 0.33) while hierarchical constraints increased by 27 per cent (to 0.19). Soldiers, as official members, have access to more resources and therefore somewhat more network range and freedom than the fully external associates. One of these useful resources available to the soldier and not to the associate is access to higher-ranked members within the family. While both associates and soldiers work under supervisors, the former are typically limited to such relations while the latter, if willing, have the advantage of forming links with established others. An associate with the potential to be made (to become a soldier) is generally sponsored by his supervisor (as N23 did for Gravano). If the sponsor succeeds in convincing higher-ranked members of the family to elevate the associate to soldier, the newly made member gains a position that allows him increasing opportunities to move beyond those offered by the supervisor.

Although remaining constrained, the soldier is able to invest more strategically in high-ranked members aside from his supervisor. Gravano, as a soldier, gradually detached himself from the clique-like crew working relationships he had held until then and began to explore new opportunities in the construction industry through the more opportune personal networks of established others. This tells us that, as a soldier, he was efficient in making the most of his inevitable constraints so as to increase his legitimacy within the family and subsequently branch out in extended social frontiers. The construction industry was that extended frontier. Fitting into the prosperous personal networks of others while increasingly expanding his own independent venturing increased the scope and variety of his relationally based opportunities. As pointed out in previous sections, Gravano's venturing in the construction industry caught the interest of the family boss, N34. While he was still under the supervision of N23, Gravano was informed that for matters concerning construction projects, he was to deal directly with the boss. The bypassing of N23 allowed Gravano to move beyond the resources directly available through N23 and towards the richer resources that could be accessed through N34's sponsoring.

Figure 5.3 shows that once Gravano ascended to the capo rank, personal network constraints dropped by 45 per cent (to 0.18) and hierarchical constraints decreased even more sharply (by 63 per cent, to 0.07). The considerable decrease in constraints indicates the increasingly non-redundant brokerage-like quality and greater network freedom that Gravano obtained in his activities. The drop in hierarchical constraints accentuates the fact that he was no longer in a position that required him to depend on a strategic sponsor for his own advancement. In many ways, Gravano had ascended to a position that made him a likely and attractive sponsor for others seeking the benefits deriving from hierarchical constraints. Gravano had become minimally constrained and therefore entrepreneurially fit. As a fully legitimate member of the Gambino family, he was now in a position to build his own social capital, and no longer strategically dependent on less constrained, better positioned members of the family. His tenure as a capo was the most entrepreneurial period in his career. Recall also that it was during this transition that Gravano's cumulative working network in Figure 5.2 began to move towards greater exclusivity.

While very slight increases in both constraint and hierarchical constraint measures were found upon Gravano's entrance into the more centralized and closed family administration as a consigliere (C = 0.22 and H = 0.09), his continuing expansion into the construction industry as well as his ability to sustain working relations with his former crew and a wide array of other lower-ranked members kept him brokering in personal network terms. Although his acceptance of this administrative role did result in a minimal decrease in his entrepreneurial capacities, it also supplemented his already privileged business and working setting with additional resources – namely, decision-making power.

The ensemble of these findings regarding Gravano's personal network capacities spanning his promotion to capo to his December 1990 arrest (at which point he held the underboss rank) illustrates the privileged relational positioning that is associated with successful careers in criminal forms of enterprise. Decreased constraints engender increased and less time-consuming opportunities (increased access to structural holes), increased autonomy in business ventures, increased attention from others also looking to get ahead, and a capacity to pursue one's activities within a more insulated, exclusive, and restrictive working network. High in opportunity and low in risk: this is the optimal working setting that privileged criminal entrepreneurs attain after years of relational manoeuvring. As is often the case, one privilege confers access to another.

6 Privileged Positioning and Access to Lethal Violence

One of the principal distinctions between Marks' independent career in the international cannabis trade and Gravano's career as a Cosa Nostra–linked construction racketeer was the absence of violence in the former and its substantial presence in the latter. The previous two chapters have demonstrated that these criminal entrepreneurs both benefited from relational forces that allowed them to advance within their respective earning activities. This chapter will consider the presence of violence, and more particularly lethal forms of violence, throughout Gravano's career. The aim here is to situate scenes of violence within the network process that has already been revealed within his promotional phases.

The role of homicide or lethal violence in Gravano's career within the ranks of the Cosa Nostra takes on the elite quality discussed in Cooney's (1997, 1998) study of homicide in modern and pre-modern eras.[1] Cooney argues that while lethal violence has been typically found to be associated with lower-status people in modern periods, it was more equally distributed throughout the social hierarchy in past 'stateless' or minimally governed societies. Following Black's (1976, 1983) theory of social control in contexts of virtual statelessness or anarchy, Cooney maintained that in social contexts defined by minimal and unequally distributed state control and a lack of third-party dispute settlers (see also Cusson 1999), high-status or elite members in past times were able to function above the law, and low-status members of the present day

---

1 Cooney defines the elite as 'individuals who have more wealth or influence than others' (1997: p. 389).

similarly must settle their own disputes because legal resort is effectively unavailable.

Lack of legal recourse may be taken as a constant in any criminal enterprise process, establishing the effectively stateless or ultra-liberal nature of such activity. Committed participants in criminal enterprise are at once capitalistic in their goals and lawless (anarchic) in their relation to conventional forms of authority and order. Lethal violence in criminal enterprise arises from competition that remains unregulated. As long as competition defines the pursuit, some form of control is necessary. Statelessness is therefore a problem within environments where competitive pursuits are encouraged. In arenas where competition is promoted and left unregulated, control is restricted to the discretion of those who succeed in remaining integral to the interests of most or all others. The regulation of competition, in this sense, becomes a resource defined by a parallel power struggle taking place within the sphere of working relations. Those who control the interests of others or who have exclusive access to resources sought after by others prevail as the competitively advantaged. Arriving at such a privileged position, as the relational analysis of Gravano's career tells us, is not a matter of an entrepreneur's ability to kill. Instead, the use of homicide in the Cosa Nostra remains consistent with the observation that 'socially prominent people in stateless societies were more assertive than most in using lethal violence to avenge insults, injuries, and killings' (Cooney 1997: p. 389). The use of lethal violence for personal purposes in criminal or stateless forms of enterprise must be understood as a privilege – a manifestation of power within a defined relational setting that embeds an activity.

The Pseudo-Hierarchy

The working environment defining a Cosa Nostra family unit is structured along three vertical allocation systems: one representing the upward flow of profits, a second representing the downward flow of sought-after resources, and a third representing the downward flow of authority and regulation. Of the three, the third is of most interest for the present discussion. The first two have been extensively discussed in the greater portion of previous analyses of Gravano's career and are the key structures upheld within the patron-client perspective in organized crime research (Albini 1971).

Anderson has maintained that observers should be careful not to confuse the economic and quasi-governance structures inherent in the Cosa Nostra family (1995: p. 40). A closer analysis of these vertical flows, however, accentuates the fact that the two (economic) allocation structures often displace the third (authority or governance). Although economic and governance allocation processes are not alike, they remain interrelated.

Such a working environment is established within a vertical, interest-based (Lupsha 1981), and situational sanctioning system defined by elite members of that system. While titles, promotions, and ranks are evident in Gravano's account, a closer look at his experiences provides little support for the bureaucratic and rigid hierarchical image that emerged from 'orthodox' conceptualizations of organized crime (Cressey 1969). While these titles and ranks are in place, they remain secondary to individual expertise and personal resources. Recall that Cressey himself expected such a shift from organizational structuring to individual resources to take place within the Cosa Nostra infrastructure. Post-Cressey studies of the Cosa Nostra (North American and Sicilian) have dismissed past forms of formal organization (Albini 1971; Ianni 1972; Arlacchi 1983; Abadinsky 1983), but have continued to stress the unchallenged authority practiced by the head or boss of a Cosa Nostra family unit (Jacobs and Gouldin 1999). The family is perceived as a 'patriarchal organization' in which 'soldiers and crews must be entrepreneurs in crime, seeking out profitable opportunities in both the underworld and upperworld' (Jacobs and Gouldin 1999: p.138).

While Gravano's account and analyses of his career do support the claim that a member's value to the family is primarily based on business and earning capacities, the dictatorial role assigned to the top echelon of the unit may be contested by considering, not simply the rules and regulations in effect, but the actual application of sanctions within the family.

In an in-depth case study of a career organized crime member (non–Cosa Nostra) in Italy, Cottino (1998: p. 89) revealed that where murder was suggested as the means of eliminating a group member, the execution could take place only if there was a unanimous decision among members. Although the working environment put forward by Cottino was based primarily on democratic principles, a link nevertheless remains with Gravano's experiences, in that what is revealed is not a totalitarian system guided by the will of the boss and defended by the traditions and rituals of a rigid, absolute governing system. Instead, the application of sanctions – most typically in the form of lethal violence –

among rule transgressors is flexible and situationalized in accordance with the influence and interests that the transgressor maintains amongst other influential members of the unit. Maltz's (1985) assessment regarding the erosion of discipline in organized crime groups throughout past decades provides a similar argument:

> Discipline within *organized crime* groups has been less than rigid. One should not expect otherwise. When all individuals in a group are armed and have no compunction about using their weapons – which may be one of the criteria for acceptance by the group – then the ability to govern them must depend to a great extent on the consent of the governed. Discipline of a group's members can be maintained only if it is shown to be in their own self-interest. (p. 29)

At the time of the ceremony officializing his entrance as a soldier into the Gambino family, Gravano was introduced to a series of rules and the basic working protocol that were to be respected by made members of the family. Obtaining permission from the family was a key element of several of the rules, as he himself explained:

> The man we answered to was our captain. He was our direct father. You do everything with him. You check with him, you put everything on record with him. You can't kill unless you get permission. You can't do anything, basically, until you get permission from the family. You don't run to the boss. You go to your captain. That was the protocol. Your captain will go to the administration of the family, which is the boss, the underboss and the consigliere. (Maas 1997: p. 87)

Further specifications of this protocol were subsequently added: 'Anytime you are sent for by the boss of your family, you must come in ... If you refuse, you will be killed ... You couldn't go with each other's wives and daughters. You couldn't raise your hands against one another. All these things meant the death penalty' (p. 88).

Formal order seems to be assured in the Cosa Nostra by the rules and capital penalties facing internal transgressors, yet Gravano quickly dismissed the reality of such ideals in looking back to his personal experiences:

> I bought this all one hundred percent. I really felt that I belonged to a brotherhood that had honor and respect. All the things I looked for in life

were in a good part of that oath. A lot later on, I got to learn that the whole thing was bullshit. I mean, we broke every rule in the book. Like, at one of the trials [for which he was a key informant after his defection in October 1991], a lawyer asked me, 'How could you break the oath of omerta?' I said, 'There's a hundred rules. We broke ninety-nine of them. This was the last rule. It wasn't that hard anymore.' (p. 88)

The structuring of order that emerges is one of neither strict rule obedience nor absolute sanctioning. While Gravano did confirm the family rank and formal title structure that was first revealed by Valachi in 1963 (Maas 1968), his prominent position within the Gambino family, as against Valachi's lower, soldier status within the Genovese family, provided a broader array of evidence concerning that structure, and in particular its flexibility. Valachi gave us an account of the American Cosa Nostra from the perspective of a stagnant, low-status member; Gravano, who experienced the Cosa Nostra from both its lower and elite levels, offers rather different insights.

Although promotional ranks do divide the Cosa Nostra family vertically, this division remains consistent with the business nature and flexibility that are themselves in tension with authoritarian practices. Vertical allotment of revenues is practiced, but authority is often challenged and questioned. Sanctions, furthermore, may be negotiated and avoided.

The Indispensable Some

Those who remain of instrumental use to influential others become indispensable to the family. Gravano, because of his network and financial resources, was among the indispensable in the Gambino family. The Cosa Nostra that was revealed throughout his account has much in common with the relationally based portrayal offered by Hess (1998) in his study of the Sicilian *cosca* (family), and is consistent with the 'crisscross' pattern of relationships that Flap (1988) saw as a key factor in determining the level of violence in an anarchic or stateless society. In a crisscross social context, one's enemy may quite conceivably be a friend of one's friend. Aggression against that enemy may therefore lead to tension between oneself and the mutual friend. Such circumstances make alternative, peaceful means of reconciliation more likely.

Gravano's strength was in his dyadic relationships. From as early as his official entrance into the Gambino family, he was in direct contact with the family boss (N34 in Figure 5.1) and other key members. Any targeting of Gravano within the family would have clearly interfered with the business activities of one or more influential family members. Although all made members may be said to have direct links to any other made member of the family, working relations call for a more important basis than mere official membership. Gravano's early and extensive endeavours in the construction industry made him a contact of interest to many other family members, and this network-based quality gave him the edge that he needed to avoid sanctioning when the threat presented itself. Two episodes illustrate this point.

In 1982, Gravano was summoned by the family boss (N34) after he arranged the murder of a flamboyant independent drug trafficker and nightclub owner (Frank Fiala) without the family's permission. Gravano, a soldier at the time, had been in the midst of selling his nightclub (Plaza Suite in Figure 5.2) to Fiala when business matters became increasingly complicated. Although reluctant at first, he accepted a bid for his thriving Brooklyn nightclub when Fiala increased the amount to one million dollars. Before the deal was completely sealed, Gravano became irked by Fiala's presence and indiscretion at the nightclub: 'I'm gritting my teeth. I tell myself business is business. Take it easy. Be quiet. Let me just get through this. Then, after that, so what? We're through with him and I got the million. I'll just swallow a little abuse. Be smart. It don't mean nothing' (Maas 1997: p. 142).

His control finally snapped when Fiala threatened him and his brother-in-law (N33) with a gun during a disagreement. Although all left the incident physically unscarred, Gravano had had enough: 'I've never been so mad in my life. As soon as we're outside, I said, "Eddie [N33], this fucker is going tonight. He should have killed me right then and there. He would've had a better shot with the law than with me"' (p. 144). This led to the first of Gravano's 'off-the-record' hits. Fiala was killed by Gravano and his crew (N2, N32, N33, N46, N47, and N48) that same night just outside the nightclub. How and why was Gravano able to avoid the consequences of this unsanctioned hit?

About three weeks after the murder of Fiala, Gravano and Louie Milito (N2: the actual shooter in the incident) were summoned to a Manhattan restaurant, through Frank DiCicco (N19), by N34. After sorting out the facts of the case and listening to Gravano's justification for not seeking permission before killing Fiala, N34 provided his final verdict, which Gravano recalled as follows: 'You're definitely not going to die over this bum. But I want your word from now on that you won't ever, ever do a piece of work unless it's approved by me, or unless somebody – and you better have the bullet holes to prove it – shot at you first and you had to kill him ... Just be a good friend of ours like you always have been. You can go now' (p. 150). This ended the Fiala incident within the family. The death sanction was overlooked in light of what the principal decision-maker, N34, took to be justifiable circumstances. Gravano, who was rapidly rising as a construction entrepreneur, was dismissed without any form of sanction.

The second occasion, not linked to any off-the-record hit, was treated as a serious internal matter that called for a more extensive hearing. The incident, in 1983, involved Louie DiBono (N52) (who in 1990 would join Gravano's list of murder victims). Once again, the dispute arose out of business dealings. DiBono, another Gambino soldier active in the construction industry, was Gravano's principal subcontractor for his drywall company (Ace Partitions in Figure 5.2). At one point, it became evident that DiBono was not paying Gravano and his partners (N33 and N49) the full amount for past contracts. DiBono was confronted and threatened by Gravano, which led DiBono to complain to his own capo, Pat Conte (not included in Figure 5.1); Conte, in turn, reported the matter to N34.

N34 ordered a sit-down soon after he was made aware that Gravano had apparently violated the rule prohibiting threats or physical aggression against made members. As with off-the-record hits, the standard punishment for such transgressions is death. The meeting took place in the basement of another made member's house. Aside from DiBono, his own capo, and Gravano, also present were N33 (who served as a witness to the episode), the family administration (N34, N35, and N36), and two other influential Gambino family members (N19 and N38). Rather than deny that he threatened DiBono, Gravano freely admitted his transgression. However, the contingent quality of Cosa Nostra justice manifested itself when N35, the family underboss, vouched for Gravano's actions as justifiable under the circumstances: 'Maybe he did wrong, but he's right' (p. 172). The matter was finally dismissed as a misunderstanding between the two entrepreneurs and resolved over a handshake.

Both of these cases illustrate the flexibility that governs the infliction of sanctions within the Cosa Nostra. While penalties are firmly entrenched within the extreme rationale of capital punishment, their application is preceded by negotiation. In both cases, Gravano claimed that his ability to avoid execution was due to his direct and honest dealings with his interlocutors. He also repeatedly pleaded that he had always had the best interests of the family and its boss at heart.

His integrity and honourable behaviour on these two occasions may indeed partly explain why he was spared the death sanction. Another possibility, which did not explicitly emerge from his personal account, is that he was too valuable to key members in the family – to his own capo and, most importantly, to the family boss and administration who received a proportion of all his earnings.

It was in the interests of the family elite that Gravano be allowed to continue venturing, earning, and expanding in the construction industry. If a criminal entrepreneur successfully maintains an entrepreneurial, brokerage-like (low in constraints) personal working network, he decreases his chances of being the target of a sanctioned or unsanctioned hit. It is unlikely that he would be removed from the network even if he develops a conflict with some of its members because he furthers the interests of others, who rely on his entrepreneurial resources. The latter save him from potential reprisals from the former.

Decision makers in the Cosa Nostra also have a stake in the profits and business aspects of the family unit. They must therefore be attentive to whose interests are being affected by the sanctioning of an internal transgressor. Aside from the obvious motivation to keep a high earner alive and earning, Gravano's life was spared on a series of occasions because he was backed by others who had interests in him and who, in turn, were of interest to the decision makers. Add the fact that Gravano was in close working contact with the family boss, and we begin to understand why he was not to be taken out of anybody's network in any way. The family's vertical allocation of financial profits, in this sense, may be perceived as outweighing its vertical allocation of authority and legitimized lethal violence. The interaction between elite interests and the flexibility/rigidity of the sanctioning system can be appreciated only when actual applications of sanctions and the decisions surrounding them are observed.

The Expendable Others

Although Gravano was able to avoid lethal sanctioning by remaining in the financial and relational interests of influential members in the Gambino family, others proved less successful in avoiding the formal implications of their personal transgressions. Figure 6.1 presents the twenty-seven murders that Gravano was implicated in to varying degrees, had knowledge of, or, more generally, was in proximity to throughout his career. Of these twenty-seven murders, which were documented in the principal and supplementary sources used in this case study, seventeen targeted made members of the Cosa Nostra. For six (lower level in Figure 6.1), Gravano had no previous knowledge of their execution. The remaining twenty-one murders had Gravano either: (1) aware of the murder before it occurred (but without his physical involvement; $n = 7$); (2) implicated in the execution of an order to kill for the family (in which he was always active in the crew assembled for the hit; $n = 6$); or (3) involved in the decision to take someone out ($n = 8$).

Only for one of these murders (victim 2 in Figure 6.1) was Gravano documented as the actual shooter. He was, however, reported as being the principal orchestrator of the hit for four (victims 6, 8, 9, and 18) and co-orchestrator for nine (victims 13–15, 20, 22–26). He was physically present at twelve murders and absent at fifteen. The top axis in Figure 6.1 tracks Gravano's rank within the Gambino family throughout his career, while the bottom axis identifies the year in which each murder took place.

From these twenty-seven murders, two forms of lethal violence emerge: *reactive* and *proactive*. Reactive violence encompasses what many criminal entrepreneurs are ready to do if provoked. Proactive violence reveals what fewer criminal entrepreneurs are ready to do to assure or increase their personal interests within a defined milieu. Reactive violence is a secondary resource that is employed when problems emerge within the boundaries of one's central business activities. If problems do not emerge, neither does reactive violence. Proactive violence, quite differently, is a resource like any other at the entrepreneur's disposal. Violence, in this proactive scheme, is the means to an entrepreneurial end.

It is easy to assume that Gravano made his way to the top of the Gambino family through the systematic and proactive use of lethal violence, and that in this he is like most successful criminal enterprise participants. The distribution of murders identified in Figure 6.1 illustrates, however, that Gravano's proximity to lethal violence increased as he rose in status within the Gambino family. This is more accurately observed in Figure 6.2, which plots the number of murders per year that Gravano was in proximity to and had at least knowledge of ($n = 21$) from one promotional phase to the next. There is a clear shift in his personal implication in lethal violence when he enters the elite of the family following his capo promotion in early 1986.

Figure 6.1 Murders in Proximity to Gravano throughout Career

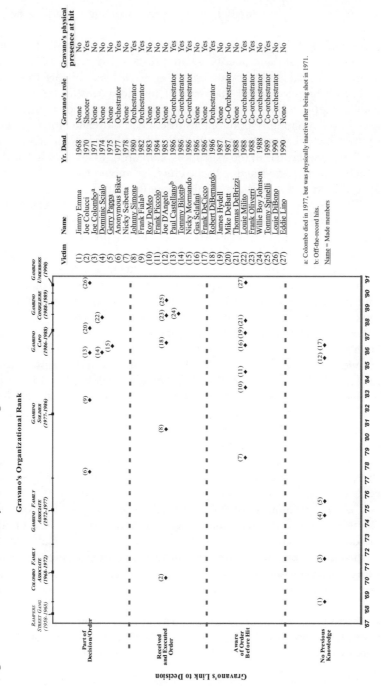

Victim	Name	Yr. Dead	Gravano's role	Gravano's physical presence at hit
(1)	Jimmy Emma	1968	None	No
(2)	Joe Colucci	1970	Shooter	Yes
(3)	Joe Colombo[a]	1971	None	No
(4)	Dominic Scialo	1974	None	No
(5)	Gerry Pappa	1975	None	Yes
(6)	Anonymous Biker	1977	Orchestrator	No
(7)	Nicky Scibetta	1978	None	No
(8)	Johnny Simone	1980	Orchestrator	Yes
(9)	Frank Fialab	1982	Orchestrator	Yes
(10)	Roy DeMeo	1983	None	No
(11)	Frank Piccolo	1984	None	No
(12)	Joe D'Angelo	1985	None	No
(13)	Paul Castellano[b]	1986	Co-orchestrator	Yes
(14)	Tommy Bilotti[b]	1986	Co-orchestrator	Yes
(15)	Nicky Mormando	1986	Co-orchestrator	Yes
(16)	Gus Sclafani	1986	None	No
(17)	Frank DeCicco	1986	Orchestrator	Yes
(18)	Robert DiBernardo	1986	Orchestrator	No
(19)	Mike DeBatt	1987	None	Yes
(20)	James Hydell	1987	Co-Orchestrator	No
(21)	Thomas DeBrizzi	1988	None	No
(22)	Louie Milito	1988	Co-orchestrator	Yes
(23)	Frank Oliveri	1988	Co-orchestrator	No
(24)	Willie Boy Johnson	1988	Co-orchestrator	No
(25)	Tommy Spinelli	1989	Co-orchestrator	Yes
(26)	Louie DiBono	1990	Co-orchestrator	No
(27)	Eddie Lino	1990	None	No

a: Colombo died in 1977, but was physically inactive after being shot in 1971.

b: Off-the-record hits.

Name = Made members

Figure 6.2 Murders in Proximity to Gravano by Career Promotions

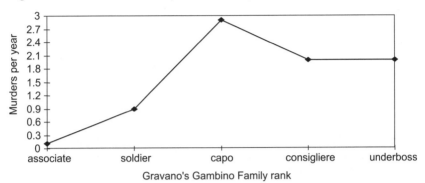

His first proactive murder was the Castellano hit (victim 13 in Figure 6.1) in December 1985. That his promotion to capo immediately followed this major event may cause some to argue that Gravano's entrance into the family elite was a result of this act of lethal violence, but, relationally, he was already in a position to assume that rank. The early 1986 capo promotion is a result of such relational strength, which, in turn, is the key factor behind Gravano's part in the assassination team to take out Castellano. Gravano's indispensability to the family was clear to both satisfied members and disenchanted-plotting members alike. Castellano's murder was a reflection of Gravano's ability to use lethal violence to benefit his own pursuits. It was his first act of proactive lethal violence. Taking out Castellano meant diminishing the constraints concentrated in his working network at that time. That he was able and invited to do so reflects his positioning within the interests of key others at that time.

As Gravano's own words tell us, misgivings about taking part in a plot to kill the family boss were not simply limited to rule transgressions that may be associated with a threat to authoritarian order. Instead, the risks of killing Castellano would come from the backlash it would create amongst Castellano's own personal contacts, who would lose a highly influential co-participant – 'I mean, this is some massive guy we're taking out, with massive connections. And we're breaking the Golden Rule. We could be looking at a war that could take eight, ten years' (Maas 1997: p. 199). Once Castellano was removed and Gravano officially entered the elite, such proactive forms of lethal violence became more common throughout his career.

A second proactive murder involved the death of Robert DiBernardo (victim 18 in Figure 6.1). Gravano took on the order to orchestrate DiBernardo's murder, justifying his compliance with a notable lack of the spirit of flexibility that had animated his defenses of his own transgressions: 'What was I going to do? What can I do? It's an order from the boss. This was the life I chose, and the boss is the boss' (p. 217). Although he maintains that the decision to take out DiBernardo was initiated by the family boss (N50), immediately after the murder of DiBernardo Gravano took control of the crucial Teamsters Local 282 (previously controlled by DiBernardo), which gave him full control of Gambino family interests in New York City's construction industry and allowed his endeavours in that line of work to progress accordingly.

Another proactive murder that took place during Gravano's privileged years in the Cosa Nostra involved his contact of thirty years, Louie Milito (victim 22). While he and Milito were partners in various criminal and legitimate ventures throughout the majority of their years together, the relation grew distant when Milito became more directly involved in business activities with the family boss, N34, and his right-hand man, N38. The death of both N34 and N38 left Milito in an increasingly isolated position within the family. Although his close working relationship with influential members of the family in previous years placed him among the more indispensable members, the loss of these two contacts left Milito somewhat expendable throughout the latter half of the 1980s. Milito, who remained a soldier, was killed because he was perceived as a threat to higher-ranked members (Gravano included). The transgression that ostensibly justified the death sanction was described as follows: 'When I became consigliere, I appointed Big Lou Vallario [N25] captain of my crew. And now Louie Milito was going around bad-mouthing Big Lou and saying he [Milito] should be captain ... This is a serious matter when a soldier is backbiting his captain. And John Gotti [N50] hears about it. We both discussed Milito. He's got to go' (p. 245). Gravano justified the taking out of Milito by appeal to the same rigid line of respect for the principles and rules of Cosa Nostra that he had applied to his earlier proactive murders: 'Louie was no innocent. He was a made guy and a killer. He knew the rules, and he went against them. He played a very dangerous game – and he lost' (p. 246). At the same time, another key, isolated Gambino construction entrepreneur was taken out of the action.

Gravano also used his privileged access to lethal violence to settle old scores with DiBono (victim 26). Approximately eight years after he threatened DiBono for not respecting a payment agreement, the two found themselves in another business conflict. Unlike the previous episode, which had Gravano facing a potential death sanction, he was now in a position to apply that sanction. Gravano sought permission from the family boss (N50) to take out DiBono. DiBono's interests in the family prevailed in the same manner that Gravano's had on the previous occasion: 'He was still robbing the family and I asked John [N50] for permission to take him out. But John had a meeting with DiBono, and DiBono told John that he had a billion dollars of drywall work that was coming out of the World Trade Centre. John bit, hook, line and sinker, and refused my request. John said he would handle DiBono personally and become his partner' (p. 249). DiBono's utility to the family boss subsequently faded when conflicts arose in that relationship: 'DiBono was up to his old tricks – double-dealing. He had obviously been bullshitting John. So when John called Louie [DiBono] in for meetings to discuss their new partnership, DiBono didn't show up. John was humiliated' (p. 249). DiBono became expendable and was taken out shortly after N50 followed Gravano's suggestion to remove him.

As a member of the family administration, Gravano was able to apply the same threat of capital punishment that he himself had faced and avoided when he was a soldier. The two conflicts between Gravano and DiBono were marked by the same general circumstances. The main difference was Gravano's more privileged positioning and DiBono's decreased importance, or expendability, within the interest-based family network.

The 'settling of an account' typifies the reactive nature of killings between criminal trade participants. Problems arise between co-participants or competitors and matters must be settled. Not all problems, as Gravano's experiences show us, are settled in a violent manner; but where they are, it is important to consider who is the target and who is applying the sanction. More broadly, to fully appreciate the lethal settling of accounts, one must first understand the relational dimensions embedding the conflict and, in particular, the victim's livelihood. Without taking into consideration the network aspects of an account settlement we cannot understand why it took place to begin with. Hence, we must consider not only with whom the target person was in conflict, but also which (formal or informal) contractual rules he transgressed and the lack of social capital that hindered his capacity to avoid sanctioning. One is expendable – a candidate for a death sanction – if no well-

positioned others see it as in their interest to stand up and offer alternative ways of settling or dismissing the account.

Network Trimming and Staying Fit

Killing is a privilege exercised by elite members in the Cosa Nostra. All
members' lives, as Arlacchi (1983) has demonstrated, are not of equal
value: 'Certain men may be killed without this calling for any condem-
nation: they are in the category of the "non-elect"' (p. 129). Not any
member may execute these expendable ones: lower-ranked members
must obtain permission to kill, and their personal interests may not be
exercised through such means. They must earn the right to use violence
to further their own interests. The privilege of using proactive lethal
violence and the expendability of a member's life are inversely related.
Higher-ranked or more privileged members may use the flexibility of
the rule and sanctioning system in their favour.

As a lower-ranking member, Gravano was involved in lethal violence
to some extent, but such participation was either reactive (whereupon
he would risk facing a death sanction) or under the order of a more
influential member (hence, in the proactive and personal interests of
elite members). Proactive lethal violence and sanctioning were accessed
once Gravano attained the capo rank and beyond in the family administration. The idea of 'off-the-record' hits became irrelevant because he
now took part in decisions about sanctioning. His use of lethal violence
for proactive purposes became legitimized within the boundaries of the
Gambino family once he entered the family elite as a capo.

Attaining a decision-making position allowed Gravano to 'trim' his
network of contacts and therefore decrease his own personal exposure.
While assuring insulation, he in no way hampered his relational capacities, in that he removed the 'less fit' of his contacts: no one that was
useful to him was taken out. Because sanctioning in the Gambino
family was neither absolute nor systematic and is explained primarily
by purposive network aspects, if one suffers the death penalty it may be
because one is a threat to the group as a whole or simply to well-placed
others within that whole; but it may also be because one has failed to
remain useful to this elite.

Interestingly, a drop in proximity to lethal violence during Gravano's
transition from capo to the administrative ranks of the Gambino family
can be seen in Figure 6.2. What needed to be done, Gravano did quickly;
he could then 'finetune' (with further hits) at his leisure. This apparent

departure from a linear association between promotions and proximity to lethal violence in Gravano's career may be better explained by the fact that the trimming process was already considerably advanced, although not fully completed.

Death sanctions against the privileged, as in the Castellano hit, are few not because the privileged are more conscientious and law abiding, but because it is precisely the privileged who decide whom to take out. Gravano's ability to circumvent the sanctioning system of the Cosa Nostra, and the differential treatment that was applied by himself and others before him, are consistent with Coleman's (1990) observation of the unequal manner in which sanctions are often applied in legitimate contexts:

> One social characteristic possessed by a potential target actor is reported by anthropologists and sociologists as reducing the likelihood that sanctions will be imposed: especially high status or power in the social system which contains the norm holders ... This provides confirmation of the view that the act of sanctioning imposes costs on the sanctioner since such costs can be expected to be especially high if the target of the sanctioning is someone with whom a continued relation is of special interest to the potential sanctioner ... This implies that even a conjoint norm, for which the targets and the holders are the same actors, may be differentially applied because of the varying costs of sanctioning different actors. The consequence is that those actors with greater power in a social system are less constrained by norms than are those with less power. There are, in fact, institutionalized excuses and indulgences available to high-status persons who fail to obey norms. A high-status person may merely be said to be eccentric, whereas the same behavior would bring severe sanctions upon a lower-status person. (p. 286)

Lethal violence does not increase one's prestige; relationally earned prestige gives one the privilege of using violence in a personal way. It is the governmental capacity awarded to higher-ranked (more prestigious) members and administrators that furnishes the means of lethal violence in criminal enterprise. Lethal violence is rooted in situational scenes of authority that are legitimized by all takers in the business exchange process. Its means are, consequently, judged by the few and applied to the many.

7 Summary and Extensions

This book was driven by an incentive to develop a framework that highlights the network properties structuring thriving careers in criminal enterprise. The assumption is that in identifying factors that promote relative success in crime, we can also infer how the lack of such factors may limit criminal achievement. A review of past research on purposive action in social networks, organized crime contexts, and more general co-offending settings, in tandem with the case studies conducted here, gives us a series of guiding generalizations that can be investigated in further case studies or tested across wider samples of offenders.

Contacts and Opportunities

In emphasizing the pivotal place of contacts throughout a career in crime, we near the opening statements of Sutherland's differential association theory. By seeing these contacts as avenues to criminal opportunities, we incorporate the basis of Merton's (1957) opportunity structure and Bell's (1953) queer ladder metaphor, while building on Cloward and Ohlin's (1960) concept of illegitimate means. Although Merton (1997) proposed various links between Sutherland's differential association theory and his anomie theory of crime, this bridge cannot be completely constructed without considering the crucial role of social capital in orienting shifts from conventional to criminal pathways, establishing a commitment and capacity for crime, and enhancing achievement therein.

Social embeddedness theory, particularly within criminal settings (Hagan 1994; Hagan and McCarthy 1997), bridges this gap more clearly.

The personal network accounts for a person's place within a wider context of opportunities. The associations that Sutherland argued were so fundamental for establishing a favourable disposition towards crime may be indicated by the opportunities to which they lead. Differential association nourishes and shapes personal opportunity structures. It accounts for the likelihood that a career is oriented towards crime because those others that make up these associations also provide the opportunities to further pursue the criminal trajectory.

Favourable opportunities are therefore favourable associations that extend from others. This is the basis for various forms of criminal sociability. Negative associations, in turn, may be given concrete form by negative opportunities or a lack of favourable opportunities. The unit of analysis is therefore not simply the individual, but the individual amongst others. The individual is perceived as taking on a personal pursuit, but such purposive action, although based on utilitarian principles, requires others to be in place in order for any form of advancement to occur.

The rise, peak, and drop pattern that emerged from the cumulative working networks in this book's case studies is precisely the pattern expected for careers in criminal enterprise that are marked by substantial length and achievement. A rise in the size of one's working network for a given activity corresponds with a rise in opportunities (albeit not necessarily the quality of these opportunities) within that activity. Criminal careers (or attempts at a career) marked by lower achievement are expected to remain flatter in network movement and more stagnant across time.

Various properties come forward at specific phases throughout such careers. Previous chapters have revealed how contacts and the network structures bounding them matter in creating the onset of such careers, in permitting their development beyond initial mentors and sponsors, and in carrying them into more privileged working settings.

Non-redundant Networking and Crime

The principal finding in the previous case studies reveals that it is not simply the number of contacts that counts, but how the structure assembling these contacts is shaped. In general, non-redundant networking (as measured by Burt's effective size, network efficiency, or network constraints) increases criminal achievement (as measured by various forms of gains or cost-avoidance).

Non-redundant networking enhances two key requirements for achievement in crime: (1) access to increased and improved opportunities, and (2) greater insulation from detection. The brokerage position is the principal exemplar of such a networking strategy. Brokers are simultaneously part of and distant from the action. Because they remain distant from that action, yet are much needed by those who take the higher risks, brokers are able to spread their participation across a series of simultaneous ventures. They have a less visible hand in, and less financial reward from, any one venture, but compensate for this by spreading available time and energy across a multitude of earning activities.

Concentrated Contact Allotment

Another important finding from the case studies concerns the surprisingly small number of key others that may bring about fundamental shifts throughout an individual's career. Concentrated contact allotment – high accumulation of eventual contacts extending from relatively few network providers – is consistent with the perennial notion of tutelage that emerged from Sutherland's *Professional Thief* (1937). In many ways, these few but fertile key contacts are akin to the mentors of crime who play crucial roles in the co-optation of future criminal entrepreneurs. This study stresses their contribution of social resources.

Both Marks and Gravano were groomed for their respective trades by incredibly few others. The seeds of Marks' career consisted of two early contacts who were crucial in providing the starting social capital that was required for him to break in and build his own place within the international cannabis trade. Gravano's network may be rooted in four key contacts, with two having had crucial roles in the early building stages of his career. In both cases, these contacts provided the required blend of limited contact (promoting security) and expansive opportunities (providing the potential for profit).

The critical building stage of the criminal entrepreneurial career depends on such key others, who offer an opportunity to get in on the action and provide resources to expand within and commit to that action. Although considerably overlooked in criminological research, such mentors are key to commitment and long-term achievement in crime.

Beyond Mentors and Makers

One assumption that was not made explicit but did become increasingly salient throughout the various phases of this study concerns the desire for autonomy that some argue to be a universal human drive (Tittle 1995). Tittle defines autonomy as 'the simultaneous exercise of external control and escape from external control over oneself' (p. 146), a feature that materialized substantially as the case studies entered the post-mentor phases of each career. This desire for autonomy is also consistent with Burt's structural hole theory, which holds that the key to success is to reduce the constraints (the inverse of autonomy) that others place on you. While Tittle stresses desire, Burt presents us with a more tangible representation of autonomy. Of course, tangible autonomy is inherent in Tittle's central concept of control imbalance.

Two kinds of movement towards autonomy emerge from the case studies. In general, Marks had to build his network by adding participants, while Gravano had to build by removing. For Marks, the objective at the onset of his career was to gather opportunities in order to create his own social capital base and be able to detach from his maker. His advancement began with very little and involved a connecting process that required him to apply his limited time and energy in an efficient manner. Loosening constraints in his network was not of concern to Marks because his activities did not take place in social settings that carried much relational weight to begin with.

Gravano, quite differently, was made in a working setting that came with substantially more relational weight than in Marks' case. Although he was not in direct working contact with all members and associates that the Gambino family offered, extensions of this power structure were ever-present. Hence, Gravano advanced in a phasal pattern whereupon a set of contacts were added to his personal network every time he progressed forward and changed sponsorship within the family. Because contacts entered his network in clusters and because not all additions were necessary, Gravano's task throughout the building stage of his career was to decrease the constraint that was added to his network that extended from the family unit.

Both Marks and Gravano maintained networks that were rooted in the networks of a select few of their contacts. They subsequently grew increasingly non-redundant in their investments in others. Marks accumulated efficiently, while Gravano cast-off unwanted constraints.

Network Closure and Privilege

All criminal entrepreneurs peak at some point or other in their careers, but not all attain a privileged position. With time and advancement, the participant who gains increasing proximity to advantageous information is able to restrict access to his own personal resources, causing a downward trend in his personal network. For the less successful, by contrast, we expect to see a downward cumulative network pattern when the entrepreneur has achieved as much as he wishes to achieve or when he confronts an uncontrollable constraint. A downward trend in the cumulative working network may therefore have two contradictory causes: (1) an end to the career, whether due to voluntary desistance, forced incapacitation, or saturation of network opportunities; or (2) privileged positioning and the opportunity to practice exclusivity and network insulation. These contexts are associated, respectively, with decreasingly and increasingly successful careers.

The career attainment phase in both of the above case studies took place when the entrepreneur was no longer obligated to seek opportunities and had become, himself, an entrepreneurial opportunity to be sought after by others. Network closure, or a decrease in the number of contacts, was an indication of the entrepreneur's shift to this privileged side of the asymmetric information grapevine. Both the quality of criminal opportunities and the level of insulation increase in accordance with the shift towards greater exclusivity. The non-redundant networking and brokerage patterns that carried the entrepreneur to this level also decrease since these strategies, which were crucial for network building, are no longer necessary once a privileged status is attained.

Networking versus Coercive Means

When we apply such relational components to our understanding of criminal enterprise, we are able to see beyond the widely accepted focus on violent and authoritarian means of advancement. As a conceptual tool, coercive means in criminal enterprise are of limited utility because they emphasize an overt criminal element over the business drive that is inherent within such activities. Traditional understandings of achievement in crime lead us to believe that criminal entrepreneurs use criminal means to gain criminal achievement. This is not the case: criminal entrepreneurs use conventional means to gain criminal achievement, but they do so in criminal trades.

This is not to say that violence, and particularly lethal forms of violence, does not exist in such contexts. Gravano's career tells us that it does, but Marks' career tells us that it is not a necessary condition. We are on shaky ground in assuming that all criminal entrepreneurs are prepared to fight, maim, or kill for their personal profit and security. In fact, when we look at conflict in criminal settings, it is surprising that violence is not more prevalent than we have been able to detect. The common thread uniting participants and sustaining collaboration in a criminal working process is mutual interest in making a living by alternative, risky, and demanding ways. Potential participants, to endure and achieve, must position themselves so as to reduce the risks of illegal activity, and must be able to cooperate with others in providing goods and services. Mutual contacts, as we saw, are also important in impeding the use of violence as a conflict resolution strategy. Any participant may of course choose violence as the means of reducing risks and obtaining cooperation; but this choice would spell not only a limited working environment for that participant, but a short-lived career as well.

As within any covert social setting, information takes on an exclusive quality. A participant cannot simply force his way into obtaining this information; he must be accepted and invited to give and take. Information exchange is consensual. This informal exchange process has some participants coming out ahead of others because they invest their cooperative resources so as to increase the exclusivity of the information to which they have access. This is a long-term investment that may be hampered or cease at any point, because the participant is not only competing for a better position within the diffusion of information, but is also competing with external legal forces looking to remove players. In such spheres of activity, the resort to violence without the backing of network strength is likely to be the result of impulse or the carrying out of an order. Violence backed by network strength, by contrast, is an indication of privilege and power over others. The use of violence is therefore not a pathway to but a sign of established success.

Organized Crime and a General Theory of Crime

The organized crime process is a long-term pursuit. This challenges the 'crime and criminality perspective' that, when applied to organized crime, argues that crime is 'incompatible' (Gottfredson and Hirschi 1990: p. 213) with notions of long-term cooperation, trustworthiness, and reliability, as well as being a creation of 'post-hoc interpretations by scholars or law enforcement officials to account for a series of events that otherwise has no inherent structure or coherent purpose' (p. 203). Ultimately, Gottfredson and Hirschi denounce the very thought of organization and crime by reducing it to a 'natural attraction to the idea that organization underlies all human activities' (p. 203). The 'naturalness' of this attraction is subsequently reinterpreted by the authors as an extension of the imperialistic influence and continuous persistence of 'sociological positivism' in maintaining a '*fully social* interpretation of the causes of crime' (p. 203).

My study addresses Marks' and Gravano's careers by demonstrating their specific capacities to shape, in their favour, the returns and risks extending from their core working networks. 'Other people' brought Marks and Gravano into their particular professions. 'Other people' were also at the root of their respective ascensions in their trades and working environments. In both cases, 'other people' continued to be key, albeit decreasing, components once each attained an established position within a prosperous network. Without these others, neither would have survived in their vocations. Purposive action approaches within the social network perspective and the basic concepts of social embeddedness and social capital allow us to pursue the classical notions of free will and choice within the environmental scope of others.

The main difference between the low-self-control version of the crime and criminality perspective and the perspective developed here is that economic action or the pursuit of self-interest is placed back into the sociological premise that has guided much of criminology. Like successful legitimate entrepreneurs, successful criminal entrepreneurs are those individuals who know how to make the most of others in advancing their goals. I therefore do come to the conclusion that crime, or at least the entrepreneurial forms of crime studied here, is 'like other rationally structured forms of human activity and can be explained in the same way: people organize to increase their safety and profit' (Gottfredson and Hirschi: p. 211).

Organized crime cannot be explained simply by individual-level features, such as low-self-control. Indeed, any such claim to a single, sufficient condition is faulty. The process of organized crime demonstrated here is not compatible with Gottfredson and Hirschi's general theory of crime. This is because continuous participation within this form of crime requires network capacities. Insulated risk-taking, adaptability, an intense belief in free competition, and an acceptance of the doctrine of materialistic accumulation are additional prerequisites that emerge from organized crime processes and remain inconsistent with the low-self-control theory of crime.

Using a network approach also overcomes another criticism raised against organized crime research: 'Apparently, it is easier to assume structure than to document it' (Gottfredson and Hirschi 1990: p. 207). By actually documenting and making network structure the analytical target of my study, I refute this claim. Structure is not assumed here; it is sought. The inquiry leads me to conclude that organized crime is not an 'illusion' (p. 213) and social organization in crime is not a myth (p. 214).

Clearly, no statistical inference is possible from my inquiry. However, Marks and Gravano do represent diametrically opposed types within the scope of knowledge that has been documented within the general field of organized crime and criminal enterprise research. The theory developed here demonstrates that, even in the midst of their evident organizational differences, both careers were built and cultivated on relational foundations. The network framework, in short, unites these extreme cases of criminal organization within a common explanatory framework. Within a general theory of criminal achievement, brokerage capacities run parallel to prosperous and long-term pursuits in crime.

Personal organization is required when performing among others. This condition cannot be stripped away in criminal contexts because it is through the overlap of personal social networks that criminal enterprise is built. Strip it away and one is indeed left with unattached individuals with very little capacity to maintain a living through crime. The problem, of course, and as demonstrated here, is that such personal social networks are there; they are just not available to everyone interested in the endeavour.

Criminal Enterprise and Criminal Markets

A social network approach to criminal enterprise avoids the assumptions driving traditional formal organizational analyses, which propose bureaucratic entities, and economic theories of the firm, which suggest images of vertical integration. This framework offers a new outlook on criminal markets. The market environments in which criminal entrepreneurs operate are suggestive of the multiscale networks described by Watts (2003) that shape trades and industries into segmented vertical systems with density increasing as one climbs towards the upper echelons.

Multiscale network structures connect the echelons, not in a formal organizational sense, but by keeping the flow of information across the distribution process flexible and robust to any external shocks. Hence, the removal of a key participant or an entire set of participants will generally have only short-term effects, since the structure is built to adapt and re-organize in response to such changes. The key vectors of information within these structures are not the bureaucratic kingpins that have so often been the target of law enforcement investigations, but the brokers who channel between clusters of groups within and across the echelons. A finding of lower density at the bottom levels of the distribution scale is consistent with the dispersed networks marking this study's criminal entrepreneurs at the building stages of their careers. As both entrepreneurs reached higher levels in their respective trades, their networks become less dispersed and more limited in number. Brokerage-like, non-redundant networking was the key to ascending through the echelons and assuming a place amongst the privileged few – not necessarily bosses, but participants with access to improved resources. Watts' insight offers us a way not only to approach structure within markets, but also to inquire into why criminal markets have proven to be so resistant to external regulatory shocks.

The underlying network dynamics that structure criminal markets and specific criminal operations continue to be exposed across a variety of trades, including illegal drug trafficking (Williams 1998; Zaitch 2002; Bruinsma and Bernasco 2004; Desroches 2005) human smuggling (Meyers 1996; Zhang and Chin 2002; Kleemans and van de Bunt 2003; Bruinsma and Bernasco 2004), stolen car trading (Bruinsma and Bernasco 2004), and fraudulent investor schemes (Baker and Faulkner 2003). The social network framework's pertinence to a wider range of criminal activities does hold much promise for identifying social dynamics within the market and beyond the group.

A Research Agenda

The approach developed in this study can be replicated. For example, a recent test of the network non-redundancy proposition was conducted by Pierre Tremblay and myself on a sample of approximately 150 money-oriented offenders that were interviewed during a prison survey on criminal earning variations. Non-redundant networking (as measured by Burt's effective size) proved to be a significant factor in accounting for increases in criminal earnings, particularly for market offenders (Morselli and Tremblay 2004).

While the basic non-redundancy issue has passed the cross-sectional sample test, other properties identified throughout this book have yet to be elaborated on a wider scale. Further case studies on a variety of criminal careers, however, will help in identifying properties not consistent with those found here or in enhancing those already formulated. What is needed, above all, are network representations of criminal career processes. New and more innovative ways of arriving at this research end can only improve the developing framework. Wider participation in such analyses would result in a research agenda that is case oriented and egocentric at each separate addition to the framework, but offers the possibility of increasing generality as more and various types of careers are subjected to increasingly systematic network investigation.

Table 7.1 displays a set of published criminal memoirs (in English, French, and Italian) that can be found in any university library[1] or new/ used bookstore (sources appear in alphabetical order by 'ego' name). Each account was written either by or with the participation of the career offender. All are excellent sources for a social network analysis of criminal life events and transitions. The wide array of criminal activities, geographical regions, and time periods that serve as contexts for each account provide a rich basis for a variety of temporal, cultural, and crime-specific comparative efforts. The list of criminal auto/biographies in Table 7.1 is clearly not exhaustive, and adding criminal memoirs published in languages and at periods not incorporated in this list would clearly expand the scope of the research agenda initiated here. Memoirs that are presented in a chronological narrative form are the most accommodating to the researcher in that the layout of events and sequences throughout the criminal career is congruent with the time-oriented analytical framework. Life histories or other biographical case studies conducted by criminologists, sociologists, or other social scientists are less feasible, since they generally place a greater emphasis on thematic or analytical partitions in the criminal career (see, for example, Shaw 1930, 1931, 1938; Sutherland 1937; Chambliss 1972; Klockars 1974; Steffensmeier 1986; Arlacchi 1992, 1994; Cottino 1998).

---

1 Such sources are usually found in the range of HV6248 or HV5805 university library call numbers.

Table 7.1 Analytically Feasible Criminal Memoirs

Ego	Author*	Title of account	Pub. year	Period of career	Geographical scope of career	Main criminal activity
Giovanni	Anonymous	*Man of Respect*	1991	1950s–80s	Sicily	Cosa Nostra (various)
John Allen	John Allen	*Assault with a Deadly Weapon*	1977	1950s–70s	Washington, DC	robbery
Robert Beck (Iceberg Slim)	Robert Beck	*Pimp: The Story of My Life*	1967	1950s–60s	Chicago	pimping
Jack Black	Jack Black	*You Can't Win*	1926	1900s–20s	United States, Canada	theft, burglary, opium dealing
Joseph Bonanno	Joseph Bonanno	*Man of Honor*	1983	1930s–70s	New York City	Cosa Nostra (various)
Malcolm Braly	Malcolm Braly	*False Starts*	1976	1940s–60s	Western United States	burglary
Charles Brooks	Trevor Allen	*Underworld*	1932	1900s–20s	England, Germany	theft, graft, pimping
Joseph Cantalupo	Joseph Cantalupo	*Body Mike*	1990	1960s–80s	New York City	Cosa Nostra (various)
Billy J. Chambers	William M. Adler	*Land of Opportunity*	1995	1970s–80s	Detroit	crack dealing (retail)
Raffaele Cutolo	Giuseppe Marrazzo	*Il camorrista*	1992	1960s–80s	Naples	Camorra (various)
Willie Fopiano	Willie Fopiano	*The Godson*	1993	1960s–80s	New England	Cosa Nostra (various)
Henry Hill	Nicolas Pileggi	*Wiseguy*	1985	1950s–80s	New York City	Robbery, drug dealing, Cosa Nostra
John Manca	John Manca	*Tin for Sale*	1991	1950s–80s	New York City	corrupt police, Cosa Nostra (various)
John B. Martin	J. B. Martin	*My Life in Crime*	1970	1930s–60s	United States	robbery
Jacques Mesrine	Jacques Mesrine	*L'instinct de mort: Récit*	1977	1950s–70s	France, Quebec	robbery
Bernard Provençal	Bernard Provençal	*Big Ben*	1983	1960s–70s	Montreal	robbery, drug importation
Michele Sindona	Nick Tosches	*Power on Earth*	1986	1940s–70s	Italy	money laundering
Willie Sutton	Willie Sutton	*Where the Money Was*	1976	1920s–60s	New York City, Philadelphia	robbery, burglary
Zachary Swan	Robert Sabbag	*Snowblind*	1990	1960s–70s	United States, Colombia	cocaine smuggler
Vincent Teresa	Vincent Teresa	*My Life in the Mafia*	1973	1940s–60s	New England	Cosa Nostra (various)
Joe Valachi	Peter Maas	*The Valachi Papers*	1968	1920s–60s	New York City	Cosa Nostra (various)

* Secondary or co-authors of these biographies and autobiographies are listed in the References section at the end of this book.

I focused on criminal achievement for the careers studied in this book. Less successful or unsuccessful careers can be handled in the same manner.[2] Through additional case studies of this sort, variations in cumulative network distributions, activities, and structural hole or other network measures can be investigated. Again, while I relied specifically on Burt's (1992) structural hole argument as an analytical and theoretical framework for studying criminal entrepreneurs, the approach is flexible enough to warrant further modifications and the inclusion of a wide array of offenders who have decided to tell their stories. A variety of analyses of criminal careers would permit a collective theoretical and empirical foundation that would further advance our understanding of the social processes structuring crime.

---

2 See, for example, Black's (2000) autobiography of his career as a thief or Pileggi's (1985) account of Henry Hill's career as an associate in New York City's Lucchese family. Both had extensive careers spanning twenty to thirty years, but neither ever really 'made it.'

Appendix A: Contact Matrices for Marks' Importation Consignments

V1-1 (Venture 1 - Consignment 1):

	1	3	19	23	25	2	11	6	10	13
N1	–	1	1	1	0	1	0	1	1	1
N3	1	–	1	1	1	1	1	1	1	1
N19	1	1	–	1	0	1	0	1	1	1
N23	1	1	1	–	0	1	0	0	0	1
N25	0	1	0	0	–	0	1	0	0	0
N2	1	1	1	1	0	–	0	1	1	1
N11	0	1	0	0	1	0	–	0	0	0
N6	1	1	1	0	0	1	0	–	1	1
N10	1	1	1	0	0	1	0	1	–	1
N13	1	1	1	1	0	1	0	1	1	–

V1-2:

	1	3	2	23	11	25	22	7	15
N1	–	1	1	1	0	0	1	1	1
N3	1	–	1	1	1	1	1	1	1
N2	1	1	–	1	0	0	1	1	1
N23	1	1	1	–	0	0	1	1	0
N11	0	1	0	0	–	1	0	0	0
N25	0	1	0	0	1	–	0	0	0
N22	1	1	1	1	0	0	–	1	1
N7	1	1	1	1	0	0	1	–	1
N15	1	1	1	0	0	0	1	1	–

V1-3:

	1	3	23	17	18	15	6	2	11	25
N1	–	1	1	1	1	1	1	1	0	0
N3	1	–	1	1	1	1	1	1	1	1
N23	1	1	–	1	1	0	0	1	0	0
N17	1	1	1	–	1	0	0	1	0	0
N18	1	1	1	1	–	0	0	1	0	0
N15	1	1	0	0	0	–	1	1	0	0
N6	1	1	0	0	0	1	–	1	0	0
N2	1	1	1	1	1	1	1	–	0	0
N11	0	1	0	0	0	0	0	0	–	1
N25	0	1	0	0	0	0	0	0	1	–

V2-1:

	1	27	12	22	3
N1	–	1	1	1	1
N27	1	–	1	0	1
N12	1	1	–	0	1
N22	1	0	0	–	1
N3	1	1	1	1	–

V3-1:

	1	3	28	26	12
N1	–	1	1	1	1
N3	1	–	1	1	1
N28	1	1	–	1	0
N26	1	1	1	–	0
N12	1	1	0	0	–

V3-2:

	1	3	11	28	26
N1	–	1	1	1	1
N3	1	–	1	1	1
N11	1	1	–	0	0
N28	1	1	0	–	1
N26	1	1	0	1	–

V2-2:

	1	3	22	11	25
N1	–	1	1	1	1
N3	1	–	1	1	1
N22	1	1	–	1	1
N11	1	1	1	–	1
N25	1	1	1	1	–

V1-4:

	1	3	23	28	22	11	25	15	19	6
N1	–	1	1	0	1	0	0	1	1	1
N3	1	–	1	1	1	1	1	1	1	1
N23	1	1	–	0	1	0	0	0	1	0
N28	0	1	0	–	0	0	0	0	0	0
N22	1	1	1	0	–	0	0	0	0	1
N11	0	1	0	0	0	–	1	0	0	0
N25	0	1	0	0	0	1	–	0	0	0
N15	1	1	0	0	0	0	0	–	1	1
N19	1	1	1	0	0	0	0	1	–	1
N6	1	1	0	0	1	0	0	1	1	–

V3-3:

	1	3	23	28	22	11	25	26
N1	–	1	1	1	1	1	0	1
N3	1	–	1	1	1	1	0	1
N23	1	1	–	0	1	0	0	0
N28	1	1	0	–	0	0	0	1
N22	1	1	1	0	–	0	0	0
N11	1	1	0	0	0	–	1	0
N25	0	0	0	0	0	1	–	0
N26	1	1	0	1	0	0	0	–

V3-4:

	1	3	2	26
N1	–	1	1	1
N3	1	–	1	1
N2	1	1	–	0
N26	1	1	0	–

V3-5:

	1	3	12	28	27	19
N1	–	1	1	1	1	1
N3	1	–	1	1	1	1
N12	1	1	–	0	1	0
N28	1	1	0	–	0	0
N27	1	1	1	0	–	0
N19	1	1	0	0	0	–

V3-6:

	1	26	28	30	7
N1	–	1	1	1	1
N26	1	–	1	1	0
N28	1	1	–	1	1
N30	1	1	1	–	1
N7	1	0	1	1	–

V3-7:

	1	26	30	29	28
N1	–	1	1	1	1
N26	1	–	1	1	1
N30	1	1	–	1	1
N29	1	1	1	–	1
N28	1	1	1	1	–

V2-3:

	1	27	22	3
N1	–	1	1	1
N27	1	–	1	1
N22	1	1	–	1
N3	1	1	1	–

V1-5:

	1	23	3	2	13
N1	–	1	1	1	1
N23	1	–	1	1	1
N3	1	1	–	1	1
N2	1	1	1	–	1
N13	1	1	1	1	–

V4-1:

	1	26	6	32	36	33
N1	–	1	1	1	0	1
N26	1	–	0	0	1	1
N6	1	0	–	1	0	0
N32	1	0	1	–	0	0
N36	0	1	0	0	–	1
N33	1	1	0	0	1	–

V4-2:

	1	26	32	36
N1	–	1	1	0
N26	1	–	0	1
N32	1	0	–	0
N36	0	1	0	–

V4-3:

	1	26	31	36
N1	–	1	0	0
N26	1	–	1	1
N31	0	1	–	0
N36	0	1	0	–

V4-4:

	1	26	11	25	12
N1	–	1	1	0	1
N26	1	–	0	0	0
N11	1	0	–	1	1
N25	1	0	1	–	1
N12	1	0	1	1	–

V4-5:

	1	12	36	26	11
N1	–	1	0	1	1
N12	1	–	0	0	1
N36	0	0	–	1	0
N26	1	0	1	–	0
N11	1	1	0	0	–

V5-1:

	1	22	11	25
N1	–	1	1	1
N22	1	–	0	0
N11	1	0	–	1
N25	1	0	1	–

V4-6:

	1	26	36	25	11	19
N1	–	1	0	1	1	1
N26	1	–	1	0	0	0
N36	0	1	–	0	0	0
N25	1	0	0	–	1	1
N11	1	0	0	1	–	0
N19	1	0	0	1	0	–

V4-7:

	1	26	36	25
N1	–	1	0	1
N26	1	–	1	0
N36	0	1	–	0
N25	1	0	0	–

V4-8:

	1	26	36	25	39
N1	–	1	1	1	1
N26	1	–	1	0	1
N36	1	1	–	0	1
N25	1	0	0	–	0
N39	1	1	1	0	–

V4-9:

	1	26	37	36	31
N1	–	1	1	1	0
N26	1	–	1	1	1
N37	1	1	–	0	1
N36	1	1	0	–	0
N31	0	1	1	0	–

V4-10:

	1	26	37	36	31
N1	–	1	1	1	0
N26	1	–	1	1	1
N37	1	1	–	0	1
N36	1	1	0	–	0
N31	0	1	1	0	–

V6-1:

	1	41	42	27
N1	–	1	0	1
N41	1	–	1	0
N42	0	1	–	1
N27	1	0	1	–

V7-1:

	1	41	42	27
N1	–	1	0	1
N41	1	–	1	0
N42	0	1	–	1
N27	1	0	1	–

V7-2:

	1	23	37	6
N1	–	1	1	1
N23	1	–	0	0
N37	1	0	–	0
N6	1	0	0	–

V8-1:

	1	41	15	6	7	32	19	26	33	39	2	38	43
N1	–	1	1	1	1	1	1	1	1	0	1	0	0
N41	1	–	1	1	1	1	1	0	1	0	1	0	0
N15	1	1	–	1	1	1	0	0	0	0	1	0	0
N6	1	1	1	–	1	1	0	0	0	0	1	0	0
N7	1	1	1	1	–	1	0	0	0	0	1	0	0
N32	1	1	1	1	1	–	0	0	0	0	1	0	0
N19	1	1	0	0	0	0	–	1	0	0	1	0	0
N26	1	0	0	0	0	0	1	–	1	1	0	1	1
N33	1	1	0	0	0	0	0	1	–	1	0	0	0
N39	0	0	0	0	0	0	0	1	1	–	0	0	0
N2	1	1	1	1	1	1	1	0	0	0	–	0	0
N38	0	0	0	0	0	0	0	1	0	0	0	–	1
N43	0	0	0	0	0	0	0	1	0	0	0	1	–

V9-1:

	1	23	45
N1	–	1	1
N23	1	–	0
N45	1	0	–

V10-1:

	1	26	40	49	33	34
N1	–	1	1	1	1	1
N26	1	–	0	1	1	1
N40	1	0	–	0	0	0
N49	1	1	0	–	0	0
N33	1	1	0	0	–	1
N34	1	1	0	0	1	–

V10-2:

	1	26	37	49	46
N1	–	1	1	1	1
N26	1	–	0	1	0
N37	1	0	–	0	1
N49	1	1	0	–	0
N46	1	0	1	0	–

V11-2:

	1	37	45
N1	–	1	1
N37	1	–	1
N45	1	1	–

V12-1:

	1	54	40	56	55	32	6	19	47
N1	–	1	1	1	1	1	1	1	1
N54	1	–	1	1	1	1	1	0	0
N40	1	1	–	0	1	0	0	0	0
N56	1	1	0	–	1	0	1	0	0
N55	1	1	1	1	–	1	1	0	0
N32	1	1	0	0	1	–	1	1	0
N6	1	1	0	1	1	1	–	0	0
N19	1	0	0	0	0	1	0	–	1
N47	1	0	0	0	0	0	0	1	–

V12-2:

	1	40	54	56	48
N1	–	1	1	1	1
N40	1	–	0	0	0
N54	1	0	–	1	1
N56	1	0	1	–	1
N48	1	0	1	1	–

V12-3:

	1	37	56	57	6	58	55	32	54
N1	–	1	1	1	1	1	1	1	1
N37	1	–	0	1	0	0	1	1	1
N56	1	0	–	0	1	0	1	0	1
N57	1	1	0	–	0	0	1	0	1
N6	1	0	1	0	–	1	1	1	1
N58	1	0	0	0	1	–	1	1	1
N55	1	1	1	1	1	1	–	1	1
N32	1	1	0	0	1	1	1	–	1
N54	1	1	1	1	1	1	1	1	–

V13-1:

	1	23	57	7
N1	–	1	1	1
N23	1	–	1	0
N57	1	1	–	1
N7	1	0	1	–

V14-1:

	1	59	58	32	37
N1	–	1	1	1	1
N59	1	–	1	0	0
N58	1	1	–	1	1
N32	1	0	1	–	1
N37	1	0	1	1	–

P1: Colombo Associate

	1	9	8	13	12	11	5	14	10	2
N1	–	100	100	37	69	69	69	1	69	100
N9	100	–	100	34	34	34	34	0	34	0
N8	100	100	–	0	100	100	34	0	100	34
N13	37	34	0	–	0	0	0	34	00	
N12	69	34	100	0	–	100	34	0	100	0
N11	69	34	100	0	100	–	34	0	100	0
N5	69	34	34	0	34	34	–	0	34	34
N14	1	0	0	34	0	0	0	–	0	0
N10	69	34	100	0	100	100	34	0	–	0
N2	100	0	34	0	0	0	34	0	0	–

P2: Gambino Associate

	1	23	16	2	24	18	25	26	27	28	29
N1	–	100	100	100	1	100	37	37	37	37	37
N23	100	–	100	0	34	0	100	100	100	100	100
N16	100	100	–	100	0	34	34	34	34	34	34
N2	100	0	100	–	0	100	34	34	34	34	34
N24	1	34	0	0	–	0	0	0	0	0	0
N18	100	0	34	100	0	–	0	0	0	0	0
N25	37	100	34	0	0	0	–	34	34	34	34
N26	37	100	34	0	0	0	34	–	100	34	34
N27	37	100	34	0	0	0	34	100	–	34	34
N28	37	100	34	0	0	0	34	34	34	–	100
N29	37	100	34	0	0	0	34	34	34	100	–

P3: Gambino Soldier

	1	23	19	32	27	2	36	16	25	33	37	26	34	38	35
N1	–	100	100	100	100	100	1	69	37	100	134	100	1	1	1
N23	100	–	34	34	100	0	34	34	100	0	0	100	34	34	0
N19	100	34	–	34	34	34	0	34	0	34	0	34	34	34	34
N32	100	34	34	–	100	34	0	0	34	34	0	100	0	0	0
N27	100	100	34	100	–	34	0	34	34	34	0	100	0	0	0
N2	100	0	34	34	34	–	0	100	34	34	34	34	0	0	0
N36	1	34	0	0	0	0	–	0	0	0	34	0	100	100	100
N16	69	34	0	0	34	100	0	–	34	0	34	34	100	34	100
N25	37	100	0	34	34	34	0	34	–	0	0	34	0	0	0
N33	100	0	0	34	34	34	0	0	0	–	0	34	0	0	0
N37	134	0	0	0	0	34	34	34	34	34	–	34	34	34	34
N26	100	100	34	100	100	34	0	100	0	0	0	–	100	100	100
N34	1	34	34	0	0	0	100	100	0	0	34	0	–	100	100
N38	1	34	34	0	0	0	100	100	0	0	34	0	100	–	100
N35	1	0	34	0	0	0	100	100	0	0	34	0	100	100	–

	1	50	19	52	20	57	60	55	56	30	33	37	49	47	59	36	51	27	46	39	42
N1	–	100	100	1	100	69	69	69	69	69	100	69	100	100	69	69	69	100	100	37	37
N50	100	–	100	0	0	0	0	0	0	34	34	34	0	0	0	100	100	0	0	34	34
N19	100	100	–	34	0	0	0	34	0	100	34	34	34	34	0	100	100	34	34	34	34
N52	1	0	34	–	34	34	0	34	0	34	0	34	0	0	0	34	34	0	0	34	34
N20	100	0	0	34	–	100	100	0	0	0	100	0	0	0	0	0	0	0	0	0	0
N57	69	0	0	34	100	–	100	0	0	0	100	0	0	0	0	0	0	0	0	0	0
N60	69	0	0	0	100	100	–	0	0	0	100	0	0	0	0	0	0	0	0	100	0
N55	69	0	34	34	0	0	0	–	100	0	34	0	0	0	0	0	0	0	0	34	0
N56	69	0	0	0	0	0	0	100	–	0	34	34	0	0	0	34	34	0	0	34	34
N30	69	34	100	34	0	0	0	0	0	–	0	34	100	34	0	34	34	34	34	34	34
N33	100	34	34	34	100	100	100	34	34	34	–	34	0	34	0	34	34	34	34	34	34
N37	69	34	34	34	0	0	0	0	0	0	34	–	0	0	0	0	0	34	34	0	0
N49	100	0	0	34	0	0	0	0	0	0	100	34	–	0	0	0	34	0	0	34	34
N47	100	0	34	0	0	0	0	0	0	0	34	0	0	–	0	0	0	100	100	0	0
N59	69	0	0	0	0	0	0	0	0	34	0	34	0	0	–	0	34	0	0	34	100
N36	69	100	100	34	0	0	0	0	0	34	34	34	0	34	0	–	34	34	34	34	34
N51	69	100	100	34	0	0	0	0	0	34	34	34	0	100	0	34	–	100	100	34	34
N27	100	0	34	0	0	0	0	0	0	34	34	34	0	100	0	0	34	–	100	34	34
N46	100	0	34	0	0	0	0	0	0	34	34	34	0	34	0	0	34	100	–	34	34
N39	37	34	34	34	0	0	0	100	34	34	34	34	0	34	34	34	34	34	34	–	34
N42	37	34	34	34	0	0	0	0	0	34	34	34	0	34	0	100	34	34	34	34	–

P5: Gambino Consigliere

	1	50	55	52	20	25	33	41	47	53	59	68	51	49	30
N1	–	100	100	1	100	69	100	100	69	37	69	100	69	69	37
N50	100	–	0	34	34	34	34	100	0	100	0	0	100	0	100
N55	100	0	–	0	0	0	0	0	0	0	0	0	0	0	0
N52	134	0	–	34	0	34	34	0	34	0	0	34	0	34	
N20	100	34	0	34	–	0	100	0	0	0	0	0	0	0	0
N25	69	34	0	0	0	–	34	34	100	34	0	34	34	0	34
N33	100	34	0	34	100	34	–	34	34	34	0	34	34	100	34
N41	100	100	0	34	0	34	34	–	0	34	0	0	100	0	34
N47	69	0	0	0	0	100	34	0	–	34	0	34	34	0	34
N53	37	100	0	34	0	34	34	34	34	–	0	34	100	0	34
N59	69	0	0	0	0	0	0	0	0	0	–	0	0	0	0
N68	100	0	0	0	0	34	34	0	34	34	0	–	34	0	34
N51	69	100	0	34	0	34	34	100	34	100	0	34	–	0	34
N49	69	0	0	0	0	0	100	0	0	0	0	0	0	–	0
N30	37	100	0	34	0	34	34	34	34	34	0	34	34	0	–

P6: Gambino Underboss

	1	50	55	52	25	30	33	41	47	49	53	20	59	62	68
N1	–	100	100	1	69	37	100	100	69	69	37	100	69	37	100
N50	100	–	0	34	34	100	34	100	0	0	100	0	0	34	0
N55	100	0	–	34	0	0	34	0	0	0	0	0	0	0	0
N52	1	34	34	–	34	34	34	34	0	34	34	34	0	0	0
N25	69	34	0	34	–	34	34	34	100	0	34	0	0	34	34
N30	37	100	0	34	34	–	34	34	34	0	34	0	0	34	34
N33	100	34	34	34	34	34	–	34	34	100	34	34	0	34	34
N41	100	100	0	34	34	34	34	–	00	34	00	34	0		
N47	69	0	0	0	100	34	34	0	–	0	34	0	0	34	34
N49	69	0	0	34	0	0	100	0	0	–	0	0	0	0	0
N53	37	100	0	34	34	34	34	34	34	0	–	34	0	34	34
N20	100	0	0	34	0	0	34	0	0	0	34	–	0	0	0
N59	69	0	0	0	0	0	0	0	0	0	0	0	–	0	0
N62	37	34	0	0	34	34	34	34	34	0	34	0	0	–	34
N68	100	0	0	0	34	34	34	0	34	0	34	0	0	34	–

Bibliography

Abadinsky, Howard (1983). *The Criminal Elite: Professional and Organized Crime.* Westport, CT: Greenwood Press.

Adler, Patricia A. (1993 [1985]). *Wheeling and Dealing: Ethnography of an Upper-Level Drug Dealing and Smuggling Community.* 2nd ed. New York: Columbia University Press.

Adler, Patricia A., and Peter Adler (1983). 'The Social Organization of Illicit Drug Transactions.' *Sociology and Social Research* 67: 260–78.

Adler, William M. (1995). *Land of Opportunity: One Family's Quest for the American Dream in the Age of Crack.* New York: Atlantic Monthly Press.

Agnew, Robert (1995). 'Determinism, Indeterminism, and Crime: An Empirical Exploration.' *Criminology* 33: 47–82.

Akerstrom, Malin (1985). *Crooks and Squares: Lifestyles of Thieves and Addicts in Comparison to Conventional People.* New Brunswick, NJ: Transaction Books.

Alba, Richard D. (1982). 'Taking Stock of Network Analysis: A Decade's Results.' *Research in the Sociology of Organizations* 39–74.

Albini, Joseph L. (1971). *The American Mafia: Genesis of a Legend.* New York: Meredith.

– (1988). 'Donald Cressey's Contributions to the Study of Organized Crime: An Evaluation.' *Crime and Delinquency* 34: 338–54.

Allen, John (1977). *Assault with a Deadly Weapon: The Autobiography of a Street Criminal.* Ed. Dianne Hall Kelly and Philip Heymann. New York: Pantheon Books.

Allen, Trevor (1932) *Underworld: The Biography of Charles Brooks, Criminal.* New York: R.M. McBride.

Anderson, Annelise G. (1979). *The Business of Organized Crime: A Cosa Nostra Family.* Stanford, CT: Hoover Institution Press.

– (1995). 'Organised Crime, Mafia and Governments.' In *The Economics of*

Organised Crime, ed. Fiorentini and S. Peltzman, 33–54. Cambridge: Cambridge University Press.

Anonymous (1991). *Man of Respect: The True Story of a Mafia Assassin*. London: Pan.

Arlacchi, Pino (1983). *Mafia Business: The Mafia Ethic and the Spirit of Capitalism*. London: Verso.

– (1988). *Droga e grande criminalità in Italia e nel mondo*. Caltanissetta-Rome: Salvatore Sciascia.

– (1992). *Gli uomini del disonore: La mafia siciliana nella vita del grande pentito Antonio Calderone*. Milan: Arnoldo Mondadori.

– *Addio Cosa Nostra: La vita di Tommaso Buscetta*. Milan: Rizzoli.

Axelrod, Robert (1984). *The Evolution of Cooperation*. New York: Basic Books.

Baker, Wayne E. (1992). 'The Network Organization in Theory and Practice.' In *Networks and Organizations: Structure, Form, and Action*, ed. N. Nohria and R.G. Eccles, 397–429. Boston: Harvard Business School Press.

Baker, Wayne E., and Robert K. Faulkner (1993). 'The Social Organization of Conspiracy: Illegal Networks in the Heavy Electrical Equipment Industry.' *American Sociological Review* 58: 837–60.

– 2003. 'Diffusion of Fraud: Intermediate Economic Crime and Investor Dynamics.' *Criminology* 41: 1173–1206.

Beare, Margaret E. (1996). *Criminal Conspiracies: Organized Crime in Canada*. Toronto: Nelson.

Beare, Margaret E., and R. Thomas Naylor (1999). *Major Issues Relating to Organized Crime: Within the Context of Economic Relationships*. Report prepared for the Law Commission of Canada. Ottawa: LCC.

Beck, Robert (1967). *Pimp: The Story of My Life*. Los Angeles: Holloway House.

Bell, Daniel (1953). 'Crime as an American Way of Life.' *Antioch Review* 13: 131–54.

Black, Donald (1976). *The Behavior of Law*. New York: Academic Press.

– (1983). 'Crime as Social Control.' *American Sociological Review* 48: 34–45.

Black, Jack (2000 [1926]). *You Can't Win*. San Francisco: Nabat/AK Press.

Block, Alan (1979). 'The Snowman Cometh: Coke in Progressive New York.' *Criminology* 17: 75–99.

– (1983). *East Side–West Side: Organizing Crime in New York, 1930–1950*. New Brunswick, NJ: Transaction Press.

Block, Alan, and William J. Chambliss (1981). *Organizing Crime*. New York: Elsevier.

Blok, Anton (1974). *The Mafia of a Sicilian Village, 1860–1960: A Study of Violent Peasant Entrepreneurs*. New York: Harper and Row.

Blumenthal, Ralph, and John Miller (1992). *The Gotti Tapes*. New York: Random House.

Boissevain, Jeremy (1974). *Friends of Friends: Networks, Manipulators, and Coalitions*. Oxford: Basil Blackwell.

Bonanno, Joseph (with Sergio Lalli) (1983). *A Man of Honor*. New York: Simon and Schuster.

Boorman, Scott A., and Harrison C. White (1976). 'Social Structure from Multiple Networks II: Role Structures.' *American Journal of Sociology* 81: 1384–1446.

Borgatti, Stephen P., Martin G. Everett, and Lin C. Freeman (1999). *UCINET 5.0, Version 1.00*. Natick: Analytic Technologies.

Braly, Malcolm (1976). *False Starts: A Memoir of San Quentin and Other Prisons*. Boston: Little, Brown.

Bruinsma, Gerben, and Wim Bernasco (2004). 'Criminal Groups and Transnational Illegal Markets.' *Crime, Law, and Social Change* 41: 79–94.

Burt, Ronald S. (1992). *Structural Holes: The Social Structure of Competition*. Cambridge, MA: Harvard University Press.

– (1998). 'The Gender of Social Capital.' *Rationality and Society* 10: 5–46.

– (1999). 'Entrepreneurs, Distrust, and Third Parties: A Strategic Look at the Dark Side of Dense Networks.' In *Shared Cognition in Organizations: The Management of Knowledge*, ed. L. Thompson, J. Levine, and D. Messick, Chapter 10. Hillsdale, NJ: Lawrence Erlbaum Associates.

– (2001). 'Structural Holes versus Network Closure as Social Capital.' In *Social Capital: Theory and Research*, ed. N. Lin, K.S. Cook, and R.S. Burt, 31–56. Chicago: Aldine de Gruyter.

Cantalupo, Joseph, and Thomas C. Renner (1990). *Body Mike: An Unsparing Expose by the Mafia Insider Who Turned On the Mob*. New York: Villard Books.

Capeci, Jerry, and Gene Mustain (1996). *Gotti: Rise and Fall*. New York: Onyx.

Chambliss, William J. (1972). *Box Man: A Professional Thief's Journey*. New York: Harper and Row.

– (1977). *On the Take: From Petty Crooks to Presidents*. Bloomington: Indiana University Press.

Clarke, Ronald V., and Derek B. Cornish (1985). 'Modeling Offenders' Decisions: A Framework for Research and Policy.' *Crime and Justice* 6: 147–85.

Cloward, Richard A., and Lloyd E. Ohlin (1960). *Delinquency and Opportunity*. Glencoe, IL: Free Press.

Coleman, James S. (1988). 'Social Capital in the Creation of Human Capital.' *American Journal of Sociology* 94: S95–S210.

– (1990). *Foundations of Social Theory*. Cambridge, MA: Harvard University Press.

Collins, Randall (1988). *Theoretical Sociology*. New York: Harcourt Brace Jovanovich.

– (1998). *The Sociology of Philosophies: A Global Theory of Intellectual Change.* Cambridge, MA: Harvard University Press.

Cook, Karen S., and Richard M. Emerson (1978). 'Power, Equity, and Commitment in Exchange Networks.' *American Sociological Review* 43: 721–39.

Cooney, Mark. (1997). 'The Decline of Elite Homicide.' *Criminology* 35: 381–407.

– (1998). *Warriors and Peacemakers: How Third Parties Shape Violence.* New York: New York University Press.

Cornish, Derek B., and Ronald V. Clarke (1986). 'Introduction.' In *The Reasoning Criminal: Rational Choice Perpectives on Offending,* ed. D.B. Cornish and R.V. Clarke, 1–16. New York: Springer.

Cottino, Amedeo (1998). *Vita da clan: Un collaboratore di giustizia si racconta.* Turin: Gruppo Abele.

Cressey, Donald R. (1969). *Theft of the Nation: The Structure and Operations of Organized Crime in America.* New York: Harper and Row.

Cross, Rob, and Andrew Parker (2004). *The Hidden Power of Social Networks: Understanding How Work Really Gets Done in Organizations.* Boston: Harvard Business School Press.

Cullen, Francis T. (1983). *Rethinking Crime and Deviance Theory.* Totowa, NJ: Rowman and Allanheld.

Cusson, Maurice (1999) '*Le Tiers exclu et la non-violence.*' Working paper. École de criminologie, Université de Montréal.

Davis, John H. (1993). *Mafia Dynasty: The Rise and Fall of the Gambino Crime Family.* New York: Harper Collins.

Degenne, Alain, and Michel Forsé (1994). *Les Réseaux sociaux.* Paris: Armand Colin.

Desroches, Frederic J. (2005). *The Crime That Pays: Drug Trafficking and Organized Crime in Canada.* Toronto: Canadian Scholars' Press.

Dorn, Nicholas, Karim Murji, and Nigel South (1992). *Traffickers: Drug Markets and Law Enforcement.* London: Routledge.

Dorn, Nicholas, Lutz Oette, and Simone White (1998). 'Drugs Importation and the Bifurcation of Risk: Capitalization Cut Outs and Organized Crime.' *British Journal of Criminology* 38: 537–60.

Eddy, Paul, and Sara Walden (1991). *Hunting Marco Polo: The Pursuit and Capture of Howard Marks.* London: Bantam.

Ekland-Olson, Sheldon, John Lieb, and Louis Zurcher (1984). 'The Paradoxical Impact of Criminal Sanctions: Some Microstructural Findings.' *Law and Society Review* 18: 159–78.

Emirbayer, Mustafa (1997). 'Manifesto for a Relational Sociology.' *American Journal of Sociology* 103: 281–317.

Emirbayer, Mustafa, and Jeff Goodwin (1994). 'Network Analysis, Culture, and the Problem of Agency.' *American Journal of Sociology* 99: 1411–54.

Erickson, Bonnie H. (1981). 'The Structure of Secret Societies.' *Social Forces* 60: 188–210.

Finckenauer, James O., and Elin J. Waring (1998). *Russian Mafia in America: Immigration, Culture, and Crime.* Boston: Northeastern University Press.

Firestone, Thomas A. (1993). 'Mafia Memoirs: What They Tell Us About Organized Crime.' *Journal of Contemporary Criminal Justice* 9: 197–220.

Flap, Hendrik Derk (1988). *Conflict, Loyalty, and Violence: The Effects of Social Networks on Behavior.* Frankfurt: Peter Lang.

Fopiano, Willie (with John Harney) (1993). *The Godson: A True-Life Account of 20 Years Inside the Mob.* New York: St. Martin's Press.

Freeman, Linton C. (1977). 'A Set of Measures of Centrality Based on Betweenness.' *Sociometry* 40: 35–41.

– (2004). *The Development of Social Network Analysis: A Study in the Sociology of Science.* Vancouver: Empirical Press.

Galaskiewicz, Joseph, and Stanley Wasserman (1993). 'Social Network Analysis: Concepts, Methodology, and Directions for the 1990s.' *Sociological Methods and Research* 22: 3–22.

Gambetta, Diego (1988). 'Mafia: The Price of Distrust.' In *Trust: Making and Breaking Cooperative Relations,* 158–75. New York: Basil Blackwell.

– (1993). *The Sicilian Mafia: The Business of Private Protection.* Cambridge, MA: Harvard University Press.

Goldstock, Ronald, Martin Marcus, Thomas D. Thacher, and James B. Jacobs (1990). *Corruption and Racketeering in the New York City Construction Industry: Final Report of the New York State Organized Crime Task Force.* New York: New York University Press.

Gottfredson, Michael R., and Travis Hirschi (1990). *A General Theory of Crime.* Stanford: Stanford University Press.

Gould, Roger V., and Roberto M. Fernandez (1989). 'Structures of Mediation: A Formal Approach to Brokerage in Transaction Networks.' In *Sociological Methodology, 1989,* ed. C. Clogg, 89–126. Oxford: Basil Blackwell.

Granovetter, Mark (1973). 'The Strength of Weak Ties.' *American Journal of Sociology* 78: 1360–80.

– (1974). *Getting a Job: A Study of Contacts and Careers.* Cambridge, MA: Harvard University Press.

– (1982). 'The Strength of Weak Ties: A Network Theory Revisited.' In *Social Structure and Network Analysis,* ed. P.V. Marsden and N. Lin, 105–30. Beverly Hills: Sage.

– (1985). 'Economic Action and Social Structure: The Problem of Embeddedness.' *American Journal of Sociology* 91: 481–510.

Hagan, John. (1994). *Crime and Disrepute*. Thousand Oaks, CA: Sage.

Hagan, John, and Bill McCarthy (1997). *Mean Streets: Youth Crime and
   Homelessness*. New York: Cambridge University Press.

Haines, Valerie A. (1988). 'Social Network Analysis, Structuration Theory, and
   the Holism-Individualism Debate.' *Social Networks* 10: 157–82.

Haller, Mark H. (1990). 'Illegal Enterprise: A Theoretical and Historical Interpretation.' *Criminology* 28: 207–35.

– (1991). 'Life Under Bruno: The Economics of an Organized Crime Family.'
   Pennsylvania Crime Commission.

– (1992). 'Bureaucracy and the Mafia: An Alternate View.' *Journal of Contemporary Criminal Justice* 8: 1–10.

Hawkins, Gordon (1969). 'God and the Mafia.' *The Public Interest* 14: 24–51.

Hess, Henner (1998). *Mafia and Mafiosi: Origin, Power and Myth*. New York:
   New York University Press.

Homans, George C. (1961). *Social Behavior: Its Elementary Forms*. New York:
   Harcourt, Brace, and World.

Ianni, Francis J. (1972). *A Family Business*. New York: Russell Sage Foundation.

– (1974). *Black Mafia*. New York: Simon and Schuster.

Jacobs, James B. (with Coleen Friel and Robert Radick) (1999). *Gotham Un-
   bound*. New York: New York University Press.

Jacobs, James B. (with Christopher Panarella and Jay Worthington) (1994).
   Busting the Mob: United States v. Cosa Nostra. New York: New York University Press.

Jacobs, James B., and Lauryn P. Gouldin (1999). 'Cosa Nostra: The Final
   Chapter.' *Crime and Justice: A Review of Research* 25: 129–89.

Katz, Jack (1988). *Seduction of Crime: Moral and Sensual Attractions in Doing Evil*.
   New York: Basic Books.

Kleemans, Edward, and Henk G. van de Bunt (2003). 'The Social Organisation
   of Human Trafficking.' In *Global Organized Crime: Trends and Developments*,
   ed. D. Siegel, H.G. van de Bunt, and D. Zaitch, 97–104. Dordrecht: Kluwer.

Klockars, Carl B. (1974). *The Professional Fence*. New York: Free Press.

Knoke, David, and James H. Kuklinski. (1982). *Network Analysis*. Beverly Hills,
   CA: Sage.

Leigh, David (1988). *High Time: The Life and Times of Howard Marks*. London:
   Unwin.

Leinhardt, Samuel, ed. (1977). *Social Networks: A Developing Pattern*. New York:
   Academic Press.

Lemieux, Vincent (1999). *Les Réseaux d'acteurs sociaux*. Paris: Presses Universitaires de France.

Lin, Nan (1982). 'Social Resources and Instrumental Action.' In *Social Structure and Network Analysis*, ed. P.V. Marsden and N. Lin, 131–45. Beverly Hills, CA: Sage.

Lupsha, Peter (1981). 'Individual Choice, Material Culture, and Organized Crime.' *Criminology* 19: 13–24.

Maas, Peter (1968). *The Valachi Papers*. New York: Bantam Books.

– (1997). *Underboss: Sammy the Bull Gravano's Story of Life in the Mafia*. New York: Harper Collins.

Maltz, Michael D. (1985). 'Toward Defining Organized Crime.' In *The Politics and Economics of Organized Crime*, ed. H.E. Alexander and G.E. Calden, 21–35. Lexington, MA: D.C. Heath.

Manca, John (with Vincent Cosgrove) (1991). *Tin for Sale: My Career in Organized Crime and the NYPD*. New York: Morrow.

Marks, Howard (1997). *Mr. Nice: An Autobiography*. London: Minerva.

Marrazzo, Giuseppe. (1992). *Il camorrista: Vita segreta di don Raffaele Cutolo*. Rome: Pironti.

Marsden, Peter V. (1990). 'Network Data and Measurement.' *Annual Review of Sociology* 16: 435–63.

Martin, John B. (1970). *My Life in Crime: The Autobiography of a Professional Criminal*. Westport, CT: Greenwood Press.

Matza, David (1964). *Delinquency and Drift*. New York: John Wiley.

McCarthy, Bill (1996). 'The Attitudes and Actions of Others: Tutelage and Sutherland's Theory of Differential Association.' *British Journal of Criminology* 36: 135–47.

McIllwain, Jeffrey S. (1999). 'Organized Crime: A Social Network Approach.' *Crime, Law, and Social Change* 32: 301–23.

– (2004). *Organizing Crime in Chinatown: Race and Racketeering in New York City, 1890–1910*. Jefferson, NC: McFarland.

Merton, Robert K. (1957). *Social Theory and Social Structure*. Rev. ed. Glencoe, IL: Free Press.

– (1997). 'On the Evolving Synthesis of Differential Association and Anomie Theory.' *Criminology* 35: 517–25.

Mesrine, Jacques (1977). *L'Instinct de mort: Récit*. Paris: J.C. Lattes.

Morselli, Carlo, and Pierre Tremblay. (2004). 'Criminal Achievement, Offender Networks, and the Benefits of Low Self Control.' *Criminology* 42: 773–804.

Myers III, Willard H. (1996). 'The Emerging Threat of Transnational Organized Crime in the East.' *Crime, Law, and Social Change* 24: 181–222.

Naylor, R. Thomas (1995). 'From Cold War to Crime War: The Search for a New 'National Security' Threat.' *Transnational Organized Crime* 1: 37–56.

– (1997). 'Mafias, Myths, and Markets: On the Theory and Practice of Enterprise Crime.' *Transnational Criminal Organizations* 3: 1–45.

Padgett, John F., and Christopher K. Ansell (1993). 'Robust Action and the Rise of the Medici, 1400–1434.' *American Journal of Sociology* 98: 1259–1319.

Pileggi, Nicholas (1985). *Wiseguy: Life in a Mafia Family*. New York: Simon and Schuster.

Potter, Gary W. (1994). *Criminal Organizations: Vice, Racketeering, and Politics in an American City*. Prospect Heights: Waveland Press.

Powell, Walter W. (1990). 'Neither Market Nor Hierarchy: Networks Forms of Organization.' In *Research in Organizational Behavior* Vol. 12, ed. B. Staw, 295–336. Greenwich: JAI Press.

Provençal, Bernard (with Bruno Boutot) (1983). *Big Ben*. Montreal: Domino.

Reiss, Albert J. (1986). 'Co-offending Influences on Criminal Careers.' In *Criminal Careers and 'Career Criminals,'* Vol. 2, ed. A. Blumstein, J. Cohen, J.A. Roth, and C.A. Visher, 121–60. Washington, DC: National Academic Press.

– (1988). 'Co-offending and Criminal Careers,' *Crime and Justice: A Review of Research* 10: 117–170.

Reuter, Peter (1983). *Disorganized Crime: The Economics of the Invisible Hand*. Cambridge, MA: MIT Press.

Reuter, Peter, and John Haaga (1989). *The Organization of High-Level Drug Markets: An Exploratory Study*. Santa Monica, CA: Rand.

Sabbag, Robert (1990). *Snowblind: A Brief Career in the Cocaine Trade*. New York: Vintage.

Sabetti, Filippo (2002 [1984]). *Village Politics and the Mafia in Sicily*. Montreal: McGill-Queen's University Press.

Sartori, Giovanni (1984). *Social Science Concepts: A Systematic Analysis*. Beverly Hills, CA: Sage.

Scott, John (1991). *Social Network Analysis: A Handbook*. London: Sage.

Schelling, Thomas C. (1984). *Choice and Consequence*. Cambridge, MA: Harvard University Press.

Sellin, Thorsten (1963). 'Organized Crime: A Business Enterprise.' *Annals of the American Academy of Political and Social Sciences* 347: 12–19.

Shaw, Clifford R. (1930). *The Natural History of a Delinquent Career*. Chicago: University of Chicago Press.

– (1931). *The Jack-Roller: A Delinquent Boy's Own Story*. Chicago: University of Chicago Press.

– (1938). *Brothers in Crime*. Chicago: University of Chicago Press.

Shover, Neal (1996). *Great Pretenders: Pursuits and Careers of Persistent Thieves.* Boulder, CO: Westview.

Simmel, George (1955). *Conflict and the Web of Group Affiliations.* Glencoe, IL: Free Press.

Smith, Dwight C. (1971). 'Some Things That May Be More Important to Understand about Organized Crime than Cosa Nostra.' *University of Florida Law Review* 24: 1–30.

– (1975). *The Mafia Mystique.* New York: Basic Books.

Steffensmeier, Darrell J. (1986). *The Fence: In the Shadow of Two Worlds.* Totowa, NJ: Rowman and Littlefield.

Sutherland, Edwin H. (1937). *The Professional Thief.* Chicago: University of Chicago Press.

Sutton, William F. (with Edward Linn) (1976). *Where the Money Was.* New York: Viking Press.

Swedberg, Richard (1990). *Economics and Sociology.* Princeton: Princeton University Press.

Teresa, Vincent (with Thomas Renner) (1973) *My Life in the Mafia.* Garden City, NY: Doubleday.

Tittle, Charles R. (1995). *Control Balance: Toward a General Theory of Deviance.* Boulder, CO: Westview.

Tosches, Nick (1986). *Power on Earth.* New York: Arbor House.

Tremblay, Pierre. (1993). 'Searching for Suitable Co-offenders.' In *Routine Activity and Rational Choice: Advances in Criminological Theory,* ed. R.V. Clarke and M. Felson, 00–00. New Brunswick, NJ: Transaction Books.

Van Duyne, Petrus C. (1996). 'The Phantom and Threat of Organized Crime.' *Crime, Law, and Social Change* 24: 341–77.

Wasserman, Stanley, and Katherine Faust (1994). *Social Network Analysis: Methods and Applications.* Cambridge: Cambridge University Press.

Watts, Duncan J. (2003). *Six Degrees: The Science of a Connected Age.* New York: W.W. Norton.

Wellman, Barry (1983). 'Network Analysis: Some Basic Principles.' In *Sociological Theory, 1983,* ed. R. Collins, 155–99. San Francisco: Jossey-Bass.

Wellman, Barry, and Stephen D. Berkowitz, eds. (1997 [1988]). *Social Structures: A Network Approach.* Greenwich, CT: JAI Press.

White, Harrison C. (1970). *Chains of Opportunity.* Cambridge, MA: Harvard University Press.

White, Harrison C., Scott A. Boorman, and Ronald L. Breiger (1976). 'Social Structure from Multiple Networks I: Blockmodels of Roles and Positions.' *American Journal of Sociology* 81: 730–79.

Williams, Phil (1998). 'The Nature of Drug-Trafficking Networks.' *Current History* 97: 154–9.

Woodiwiss, Michael (2001). *Organized Crime and American Power: A History.* Toronto: University of Toronto Press.

Zaitch, Damián (2002). *Trafficking Cocaine: Colombian Drug Entrepreneurs in the Netherlands.* The Hague: Kluwer.

Zhang, Sheldon, and Ko-lin Chin (2002). 'Enter the Dragon: Inside Chinese Human Smuggling Operations.' *Criminology* 40: 737–67.

Index